Editor's Introduction
The Portrait Issue

This issue of *BJP* focuses on portraiture, partly to highlight our 2023 Portrait of Humanity series winners [page 142], but also because in portraiture the politics of representation stand out. Who photographs what, how and why are perennial questions, but they are most pertinent when people are being depicted – and when those people are clearly identifiable. Visibility can feel like acknowledgement, an important step towards social and political justice. But it can also swing the other way, towards being tracked or stereotyped, singled out for derision or worse.

Thinking in this area is evolving, as the new publication *Collaboration* shows. Put together by two photographers and three academics, it retells the history of images by giving the subjects as much weight as the image-makers. "The root of my ambivalence about photography, right from the beginning, was the power of the camera over and in the act of representation," says Susan Meiselas [page 106]. Meanwhile, in our cover feature, Mickalene Thomas creates new representations of Black women, arguing that it is important to "explore a transformative way of how we can see ourselves" [page 70].

Camille Gharbi opts not to show her subjects' faces when depicting both aggressors and survivors of domestic violence [page 84]. Visiting a refuge for young women, she maintains anonymity for those who have had to rebuild their identities and lives. In photographing those who have killed, she suggests the disturbing ubiquity of the Everyman, and of this kind of aggression. "Domestic abusers cannot just be recognised at will," points out writer Sarah Moroz. "When a certain kind of violence is endemic, the point is that it is widespread."

For Queer image-makers, photography can help create a space to exist, providing "proof of existence in a world in which law and institutions continue to deny our fundamental human rights", writes Gem Fletcher [page 114]. With this in mind, *BJP* has offered space to Save the Children to talk through its use of images from the conflict in Gaza and Israel [page 11]. At the time of writing, the violence is ongoing, and children are suffering its most brutal consequences. *BJP* commends Save the Children for its efforts to responsibly use – and not use – photography to advocate for these innocent victims.

Diane Smyth
Editor

B

Daniel Meadows Book of the Road

Book of the Road celebrates the 50th anniversary of Daniel Meadows'
pioneering 1970s documentary project the Free Photographic Omnibus.

Driving over 10,000 miles in a double-decker bus, the wild-haired
young Meadows spent 14 months mapping the length and breadth of
England, photographing 958 people and offering a free print to each of his
subjects. Along the way, amongst countless breakdowns, parking tickets
and random acts of kindness, he had chance encounters with the likes of
Led Zeppelin's Robert Plant.

"This country is changing quickly... we might soon forget those interesting
relics of the past that are disappearing under the redevelopment of the future."
This future is now here, and Meadows' pictures remain as relevant as ever.
Book of the Road cements the Free Photographic Omnibus as an essential
document of 1970s England – an urgent and timeless visual record. Meadows'
determination allowed him to assemble all this material into a cartographic
census of an evolving nation.

Contents

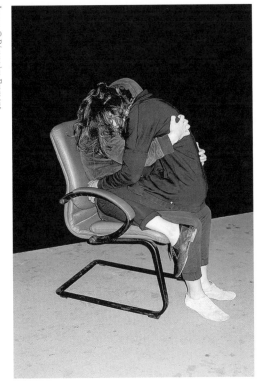

114

Queer New Wave

How does portraiture help build communities, both in images and in practice? Gem Fletcher discusses with Bérangère Fromont, Myriam Boulos, Janina Sabaliauskaitė, Jesse Glazzard and Devyn Galindo.

128

The Commissioners

Three photo commissioners talk through what makes a good editorial portrait – Emma Bowkett, director of photography at *FT Weekend Magazine*; Andreas Wellnitz, consultant for *ZEITmagazin*; and Jonny Lu, creative director for *i-D*.

Cover image: *Clarivel with Orange Earring*, 2015 © Mickalene Thomas.

The Portrait Issue, Issue 7916, Volume 170, ISSN: 0007-1196

Elisa Medde

With a background in art history, iconology and photographic studies, Elisa Medde's research reflects on the relationship between image, communication and power structures. From 2012 to 2023, she was editor-in-chief of *Foam Magazine*. She has nominated for various prizes including the Luma Rencontres Book Award and Prix Elysée, and she lectures at the École cantonale d'art de Lausanne. Her writing has appeared in *Flash Art*, *Photo-Eye*, *Something We Africans Got*, *Vogue Italia* and others.

@elsmdd

Emma Shapiro

Emma Shapiro is an artist, writer and activist dedicated to advocating for artists facing online censorship. She is editor-at-large for the Don't Delete Art campaign, providing resources, support and education for at-risk artists. Passionate about building community and sharing information, Shapiro founded the international art project and body equality movement Exposure Therapy. She also writes widely on art censorship, digital rights and feminism.

emma-shapiro.com

Alice Zoo

London-based photographer and writer Alice Zoo explores ritual and meaning-making in contemporary Britain – and the ways in which image and text enrich and complicate one another. She works on commission for publications including *National Geographic* and *The New Yorker*, and her images have been exhibited at the National Portrait Gallery and the Royal Photographic Society. She writes regularly for Magnum Photos, and publishes *Interloper*, a monthly photography newsletter.

alicezoo.com

Diane Smyth

Diane Smyth rejoined *BJP* as editor in early 2023. She started at the magazine in 2003, working in various editorial roles until 2018, when she went freelance. She is also the editor at Photoworks, where she recently edited *Photoworks Annual #30, The Thing*. Smyth's writing has appeared in *Aperture, Trigger, The Art Newspaper, Apollo, The Guardian* and *FT Weekend Magazine*. She is an associate lecturer at London College of Communication, where she teaches photography theory and history.

@dismy

Editor
Diane Smyth

Deputy editor
Ravi Ghosh

Editor-at-large
Simon Bainbridge

Creative director/CEO
Mick Moore

Chief sub-editor
Kathy Ball

Staff writer
Philippa Kelly

Digital marketing manager
Giulia Salerno

Chief designer
Nicky Brown

Head of awards production
Zoe Harrison

Finance director
Mark Bounds

Editorial
editorial@1854.media

Subscriptions & membership enquiries
subscriptions@1854.media

Advertising, distribution & marketing
marketing@1854.media

1854.photography

1854

Published by 1854 Media Ltd ©
1854 Media Ltd, Crowmeole Barn,
Crowmeole Lane, Shrewsbury,
Shropshire, England, SY3 8AY. UK
Company No: 8361351.

Contributors

In Agenda, we speak to Save the Children UK about its use of imagery, An-My Lê talks through her MoMA showcase, and we preview festivals from south-east China to the banks of the Rhine. Plus Micaiah Carter is our Spotlight artist and Sabina Jaskot-Gill is in Any Answers

Agenda

As the conflict in Israel and Gaza continues, Ivy Lahon from Save the Children UK discusses the role photography can play in communicating aid efforts and advocating for human rights

Appealing for aid

Founded in the UK in 1919, Save the Children is now based in 115 countries and employs around 24,000 people. The organisation is currently running a Gaza Emergency Appeal to help children caught up in the conflict in Israel and Gaza, and communications around this appeal in the UK are being overseen by Ivy Lahon, head of creative content and stories. *BJP* caught up with Lahon at the start of November to find out more about this campaign and Save the Children's work.

How does Save the Children UK communicate?

Social media – such as Instagram, Facebook, TikTok, YouTube, Twitter or LinkedIn – is one of our most visible platforms, but there are a multitude of ways. This could be to new and existing supporters, to our partners, volunteers, institutions, or the UK government. Our communication channels span email, our website, printed letters, our retail shops, events, press ads or articles in national or global editorials.

Our comms for the Gaza Emergency Appeal have been no different to other appeals, however we have seen high engagement rates on social media. I think this is due to the nature of the conflict and the exceptional circumstances surrounding its emergence, and the degree of violence and suffering that has taken place on both sides.

How important is photography to fundraising efforts?

Photography and authentic storytelling are crucial to fundraising communications in any emergency, including the Gaza Appeal. A powerful set of images can create a deep connection and evoke strong emotions, as well as informing audiences on what Save the Children is doing to help. However, receiving photography, video or any first-hand testimony during this crisis has been incredibly challenging due to the live nature of the conflict – and while the safety and security of our staff in Gaza is a clear priority. As part of our commitment to uphold the dignity of contributors above all else, we avoid showing identifiable images unless we're able to carry out a robust informed consent process, which is very hard to do in an unfolding crisis.

Both these factors mean we've used more graphic, text-led posts featuring statistics or quotes as well as illustrations for the Gaza Appeal. In the absence of our own content in the first few days – and when the situation was unclear – one of our first posts featured the quote, 'Every war is a war against children' from our founder Eglantyne Jebb, and an illustration by Andrés Landazábal [3]. We've since commissioned two illustrations with Andrés for the Gaza Appeal which we'll use across channels. One features a queue of children waiting for food and water, while the other shows a pregnant woman fleeing an air strike with her infants.

1

1 A child's chair among the rubble in Gaza © Bisan Owda/Save the Children.

2 On 31 Oct, the message 'Ceasefire Now' and an image of a child were projected onto the Houses of Parliament, in a project led by Save the Children and supported by Oxfam, Action Against Hunger and Catholic Agency for Overseas Development.

3 Images from Save the Children UK's Gaza Emergency Appeal. Top left: Illustration by Andrés Landazábal, quote by Eglantyne Jebb; Top right: Image © Majdi Fathi/NurPhoto/Getty Images; Bottom right: Image © Abed Rahim Khatib/Andadolu/Getty Images.

The United Nations Population Fund (UNFPA) estimates there are currently 50,000 pregnant women in Gaza, of whom 5500 are expected to deliver in the next month and are unable to obtain basic health services. Gaza's one million children have been cut off from the basics they need to survive, with very limited access to clean water, leaving them at risk of dying from severe dehydration, and with food and medicines running out fast.

Is it possible to remain neutral when advocating for aid? Is calling for a ceasefire partial?

As well as being an organisation that provides humanitarian aid, Save the Children is a campaigning organisation which lobbies governments on policy and proactively advocates for the rights and needs of the people we support. Save the Children is calling for an immediate ceasefire in the Gaza Strip and Israel to prevent a humanitarian catastrophe and further loss of innocent lives. We have witnessed unfathomable death and destruction in which thousands of people have been killed, injured, displaced, and nearly 250 Israelis remain held hostage, including children and the elderly.

The number of children reported killed in Gaza in just three weeks has surpassed the annual number of children killed across the world's conflict zones since 2019, and this number is still rising. Palestinians in search of safety have nowhere to go. Children are always the first to suffer and pay the heaviest price in any conflict. All children should be protected and Save the Children is calling on world leaders to use their influence and demand an immediate ceasefire so every effort can be made to ensure children and civilians receive humanitarian relief immediately.

Is Save the Children still able to use photography when, for example, Gaza does not have internet?

Communication blackouts, as well as prioritising the safety of comms staff, has meant so far we've received limited photography and footage from Gaza. We're also not able to deploy a photographer into the area (which is what we'd normally do if local staff aren't able to shoot), so we've licensed some news agency images, for example for our Emergency Appeal hero image. If used carefully, considerately and only when necessary, newswire images can help us show the situation for children and families when we're not able to gather content ourselves.

Where does Save the Children get its photographs?

We work with local, regional and international photographers, with an emphasis on hiring local and regional where we can. Using local photographers can mean an understanding of languages, issues, or cultural subtleties which helps build rapport, trust and connection with the communities we support. It's not always appropriate or possible to hire locally however, and our priority is always the welfare of children and

families we feature – and ensuring the person gathering their story has experience working sensitively or in challenging situations.

How do you balance urgency with accuracy and reflection?
Speed-to-market in an emergency is important, but we have stringent checks and sign-off procedures to adhere to, so accuracy, reflection, and the consent and dignity of the subjects are never compromised, no matter the urgency. Typically, in an emergency, if we have the content, we can publish something within a few hours, even with the Gaza Appeal.

Do people have to be shown suffering to provoke pity?
There is an ongoing debate in the sector about hard-hitting fundraising imagery and a myth that in order to evoke a response, you must show extreme suffering. This can be problematic in the fundraising space, especially when communicating about hunger, for example, because it can lead to stigmatisation, 'othering' or negative stereotyping of communities who are only shown as passive victims or in a context of need or suffering. Images such as children playing in a shelter in southern Gaza are important to include, not only because they show Save the Children's work and impact, but also because they humanise people involved in an emergency, reminding audiences that children are children wherever they are and whatever they are experiencing.

In most emergencies the public sees harder-hitting imagery in news media. It's not always our role to show extreme suffering that is already in the public sphere, but to highlight the human story, the nuance and detail of lives and experiences, as well as Save the Children's impact and how our support can make lasting change.

Does the idea of compassion fatigue impact the imagery used?
Guilt-inducing communications that leave audiences feeling situations are hopeless or futile don't inspire them to act. We know audiences respond much better to storytelling that shows hope or potential, and that one way to close the empathy gap is to highlight the universal, common or relatable in all of us. This means avoiding showing people in extreme distress, not only

Illustration: Andrés Landazábal / Save the Children UK

Photo: Majdi Fathi / Nur Photo via Getty Images

STOP THE WAR ON GRANDMOTHERS.
STOP THE WAR ON GRANDFATHERS.
STOP THE WAR ON MOTHERS.
STOP THE WAR ON FATHERS.
STOP THE WAR ON SISTERS.
STOP THE WAR ON BROTHERS.
STOP THE WAR ON DAUGHTERS.
STOP THE WAR ON SONS.
STOP THE WAR ON CHILDREN.

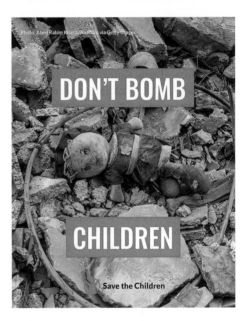

Photo: Abed Rahim Khatib/Anadolu via Getty Images

because it can perpetuate a negative stereotype by reducing a person's story to their moment of crisis, but also because it's harder to engage audiences.

Are there any images Save the Children will not show?
We have robust image guidelines that safeguard against harm to anyone in our communications. For example, we anonymise stories if identification might be a risk to the child, such as cases of ex-child soldiers, unaccompanied minors or survivors of sexual violence. This also includes harm from stigmatisation, so images which show extreme distress with partial nudity and no context of care, that perpetuate a negative single side of a story, are also avoided.

Has the imagery circulating from Gaza differed from other conflicts?
Social media has changed the way the public consumes information about emergencies. Content about crises once appeared in newspapers or websites only, but now Instagram, TikTok and other social media platforms provide live updates from citizen journalists as conflicts or disasters unravel. Unfortunately, the images we've seen from Gaza over the last few years have been consistently harrowing, but social media and the democratisation of information sharing has played an interesting role in this latest escalation where the public is able to see first-hand how the situation develops from day to day. **BJP**

savethechildren.org.uk

GULF
PHOTO
PLUS

**THE MIDDLE EAST
AND NORTH AFRICA'S
DESTINATION FOR
PHOTOGRAPHY.**

Gulf Photo Plus is a community organization
and the region's leading photography center.

We cultivate visual practices through year-
round workshops, art programs, exhibitions,
community events, and state-of-the art
printing services and specialized resources.

Image from the Opening of *Swallow This:
Arab Women and Body Politics*, by Lara
Chahine and Reem Falaknaz, 2021.

Find out more at gulfphotoplus.com.

Heavily influenced by the Vietnam War, An-My Lê probes the fears and fictions behind our militarised era. This major solo show sees her loop history into new cycles, finds Ravi Ghosh

Between Two Rivers

Defining the relation between An-My Lê's work and war is complex. Rather than a theme, preoccupation or subject, the Vietnamese American photographer describes conflict as an "underpinning", a foundation from which many divergent experiments flow. "War becomes not a singular cataclysmic event, but a quotidian mode of existence that structures our social and affective lives," reflects Roxana Marcoci, MoMA's acting chief curator of photography. *Between Two Rivers/Giua hai giòng sông/Entre deux rivières* puts this mode of existence on

display in the heart of the US cultural establishment, using photography to highlight the self-delusions and raw power of a militarised American state – and on perceptions of Vietnam today.

Lê's personal experience of the Vietnam conflict and its legacy "is why I make work," she says. Growing up in Hue and Saigon, she arrived in the US as a political refugee in 1975, studying biology at Stanford University before pursuing an MFA at Yale School of Art. When diplomatic relations eased under the Clinton administration, Lê returned to Hanoi and the Mekong Delta, making

1

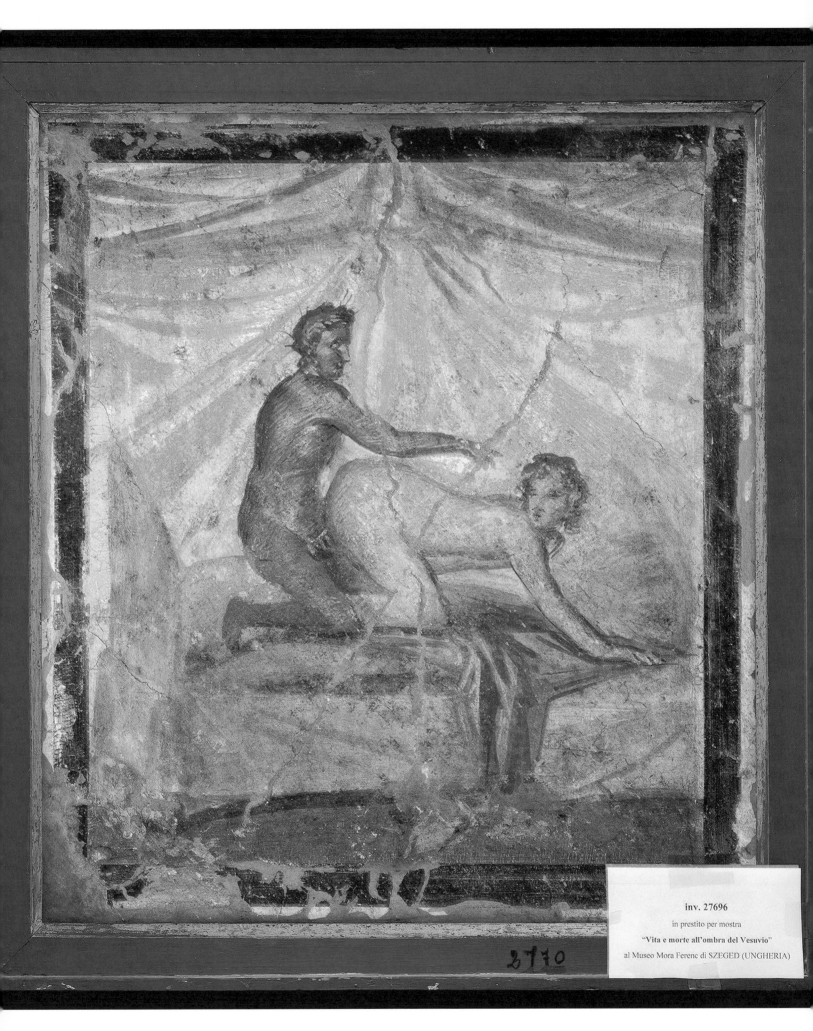

inv. 27696

in prestito per mostra

"Vita e morte all'ombra del Vesuvio"

al Museo Mora Ferenc di SZEGED (UNGHERIA)

3

quiet, large-format landscape photographs which propelled her artistic career. War is absent, but the diplomatic context, and Lê's own migrations, create an intrigue which the *Viêt Nam* pictures match in their detail. In one, we scan the walls of a Bac Giang home for signs of the north's past, but find instead a scene frozen in time, an old sewing machine, cacti, busts and a mid-century sideboard filling the frame.

The exhibition title foregrounds the artistic and social relationship Lê has maintained between the Mississippi and the Mekong. *Delta* (2011) shows Vietnamese women in New Orleans and Ho Chi Minh City, vibrant colour portraits that emphasise similarity as well as difference. New York City is home to around 20,000 Vietnamese Americans, 60 per cent of whom were born abroad. Showing these works at MoMA speaks to Lê's global consciousness; she mentions the dislocation of diaspora life, as well as the shakiness of the US' democratic experiment. "Living through the war

and being a refugee continues to reverberate today with immigrants from Latin and South America," she says. Her past becomes a vehicle for empathy, the photographs public tokens of solidarity.

Lê spent the period between 1999 and 2004 tracing the ways in which war is alive in the American psyche, whether real or imagined, imminent or deferred. In Virginia and North Carolina, she photographed men who re-enact the Vietnam conflict for *Small Wars*, while in the arid Californian desert, she made intense studies of military training exercises on the eve of the Afghanistan and Iraq wars for *29 Palms* (2003–04) [5]. Films relating to both series appear at MoMA. *Events Ashore* [1 & 3] shows the prowess of the US Navy, the colour shots gesturing towards a sense of misplaced adventure. (Lê was invited onboard by a colonel). People often ask whether she is fetishising the military. "Of course not," she tells me. "People throwing that word around without understanding

what it means" motivated her to explore the history of erotic imagery, the thin line which can separate desire and violence. *Gabinetto* (2016) [2] – pictures of erotic artefacts from Naples' Secret Museum – and new porn-inspired embroideries explore this at MoMA.

While visiting her mother in Orange County during the pandemic, Lê began returning to the Twentynine Palms training base, nearly two decades after she first observed exercises there. She had access to a raised viewing point, the swirling dust drifting across the desert as it had done in her black-and-white shots of mortars and gun drills. "I had a quasi out-of-body experience and remembered why I was there," Lê recalls. "I saw the span of my mother's life flashing across the landscape, from her birth in Hanoi in the early 1930s and through various occupations." Lê's mother had been awarded a scholarship to study in France in the 1950s, returning to a divided Vietnam after the Geneva Accords in 1954. But her health was now deteriorating, accelerated by

1 *Manning the Rail, USS Tortuga, Java Sea*, from the series *Events Ashore*, 2010.

2 *Erotic Scene (from the Lupanar of Pompeii), National Archaeological Museum of Naples*, from the series *Gabinetto*, 2016.

3 *Sailors on Liberty from USS Prebble, Bamboo 2 Bar, Da Nang, Vietnam*, from the series *Events Ashore*, 2011.

4 *High School Students Protesting Gun Violence*, from the series *Silent General*, 2018.

5 *Security and Stabilization Operations, Graffiti I*, from the series *29 Palms*, 2003–04.

All images © An-My Lê. Courtesy of the artist and Marian Goodman Gallery.

4

An-My Lê: Between Two Rivers/Giua hai giòng
sông/Entre deux rivières is at the Museum of
Modern Art, New York until 16 March 2024.
moma.org

5

Covid isolation. "She would shuttle back and forth with this fragmented life defined by American geopolitics – which was also my life," Lê says. As the vision faded, helicopters circled and another training exercise began.

Lê describes the experience as confusing, but was struck by the power of a 360-degree vista. She began discussing the potential for a new immersive work with Marcoci. The resulting installation, *Fourteen Views*, consists of vertical panels stitched together from Lê's "library of clouds", inspired by the work of JMW Turner and the sublime. The cyclorama is derived from negatives, but Lê used Photoshop and other digital tools to stitch images together, a departure from her typical hands-off approach. The new work helps answer a genre query often put to Lê, whose method is sometimes compared to photojournalism or documentary. "There was always this question of 'Where's the art?' and 'Where does the art reside?' in my work," she says. "It's an open question… with Thomas Demand, you know where the art is."

Between Two Rivers showcases Lê's mixed-media practice in a way that her first US institutional solo show did not. *On Contested Terrain* featured more than 125 photographs organised in juxtaposing series clusters, opening in 2020 at Pittsburgh's Carnegie Museum of Art before travelling to Fort Worth and Milwaukee, concluding in March 2022. Speaking now, Lê views the show as something of a research exercise in anticipation of a more experimental outing. "That idea of looking at the work on the wall is always very clarifying," she explains. "I was able to see clearly the connections between my ideas and my concerns throughout projects – some are different iterations; some are completely new ideas; and some are extensions."

This makes the MoMA show a pivotal moment, a chance to disrupt a linear way of looking, whether via series mash-ups, embroideries or digital alterations. *Silent General* (2015–ongoing) [4] epitomises this; a roving, agile series suitable for state-of-the-nation *New York Times* picture essays and shots of high-school students alike. The work moves in motion with the country, as it did when debates around the southern border shifted either side of Trump's election in 2016. The task at MoMA is to capture that variety without drifting. "I'm thinking about what it means to group together a multitude of pictures inspired by poetics, rhythms, dissonance and breaks – remembering the first image and carrying that impression on to the next photograph," she observes. Lê's mindset suits river flow or current analogies. "I've been around long enough to see that history is cyclical," she says. "We always talk about how the Vietnam War was a lesson learned, but it wasn't." BJP

anmyle.com

Now in its ninth year, the Chinese festival brings works from Les Rencontres d'Arles alongside its own cutting-edge programme. Diane Smyth speaks with co-founder RongRong

Jimei × Arles International Photo Festival

On 15 December 2023 the Jimei × Arles International Photo Festival opens in Xiamen, south-east China, the ninth time it has returned to the port city district. Open until 21 January 2024, it features 32 exhibitions by artists from France, the US, Scandinavia, China, Taiwan, Hong Kong, Bangladesh, Cambodia and many more, with shows relocating from the 2023 Les Rencontres d'Arles, and others dedicated to emerging Chinese artists, and photography and moving-image curators. The opening weekend will also include portfolio reviews, lectures, workshops, artist tours and performances.

This year Jimei × Arles replaced the role of art director with an art committee, featuring Christoph Wiesner, director of Les Rencontres d'Arles; Gu Zheng, photography critic; Gwen Lee, co-founder of the Singapore International Photography Festival and founding director of DECK; Yan Qi, executive director of Three Shadows Photography Art Centre; and RongRong, contemporary photographer and co-founder of Three Shadows and the Jimei × Arles festival, who together curated the programme and some of the shows. "We do not give each year's festival a specific theme," RongRong explains. "We encourage diversity and welcome exhibitions from different countries and cultures. We hope to see everyone's uniqueness."

The festival has several sections in which to explore different aspects of photography. *Exhibitions from Arles* brings international work from the 2023 French festival to a Chinese audience, and includes the publications shortlisted for Arles' Book Award. The committee selected the Wim Wenders exhibition *My Polaroid Friends*, as well as part of the *Søsterskap (Sisterhood)* Contemporary Nordic Photography show, *Hoja Santa (Holy Leaf)* by Maciejka Art, and the moving-image work *Cosmovisión* by Garush Melkonyan. Jimei × Arles will also feature two shows

taken from the Rencontres d'Arles Discovery Award, which was curated by Tanvi Mishra: *Caribbean Dreams* by Samantha Box [featured in *BJP* #7915], and *The Ajaib Ghar Archive* by Philippe Calia [6].

"For Chinese audiences to visit Les Rencontres d'Arles in France, the costs of airfares and accommodation are high," says RongRong. "Having these works brought to our doorstep provides a fantastic opportunity for local audiences.

"Les Rencontres d'Arles in France is the pioneer of photography festivals and has been held for over 50 years, showcasing numerous international artists," he adds. "Three Shadows Photography Art Centre is extremely honoured to have the opportunity to collaborate with such a prestigious national art event."

Jimei × Arles is a two-way relationship with the French festival, with the winning exhibition from the Jimei × Arles Discovery Award receiving 100,000 yuan plus a showcase in next year's Les Rencontres d'Arles. This award highlights emerging image-makers from China, with eight artists nominated by four curators – this year, Chen Min, Joanna Fu, He Bo and Yao Siqing. They have chosen, respectively: Li Dan for the series *Samples of Air*; Liu Guangli, *Katabasis* [2]; Lahem, *Modernity's Fracture: The Odyssey of Returning Hometown*; Wu MeiChi, *Baby's Baby* [4]; Wu Yuhang, *Fragmentary*; Zhang Lanpo, *A Multitude of Riddles, in Stasis, in the Open*; btr, *AIR*; and Yu Guo, *Layered Views*.

The works cover a broad variety of subjects and approaches, from Wu MeiChi's wild digital interventions and Liu Guangli's experiments in AI and 3D modelling, to Lahem's delicate images of his hometown, a small village in the southern mountains of Jiangxi. RongRong says he is always curious to see the series picked out for the Discovery Awards, adding that there has been a notable increase in work

2

using new media or multimedia approaches in recent years – a shift he links to the fast pace of development in imaging technology. He hopes Jimei × Arles represents younger cohorts of Chinese artists, and ensures those voices are heard internationally. "When visiting Les Rencontres d'Arles, we noticed that the voice of Chinese photography is relatively weak," he notes. "It is highly significant for the works of our photographers to be exhibited at Arles alongside artists from other countries."

New technology

Jimei × Arles is also highlighting cutting-edge thinking via *China Pulse*, a section devoted to a different Chinese art institution every year. For 2023 it is welcoming Tsinghua University's Academy of Arts & Design, with the section titled *Forever Young* after the university's motto. The show is divided into two parts, *Literature and Performance* and *Fiction and Experiment*, and draws on Tsinghau University's 30-year history of photographic education – an unusually long history in China, where photography majors have only been established for the last 20 years. Tsinghau started teaching photography in 1991 and set up its first photography major in 2010, emphasising interdisciplinary work and making the integration of art and science a cornerstone.

Curated by Feng Jianguo, *China Pulse*'s range of artists includes RongRong, as well as Gao Yuan, Lei Lei and Wang Shiran – whose works create uncanny updates of icons of the western photographic canon. "When reflecting on the history of world photography art spanning nearly two centuries, it's clear that this narrative has evolved atop a foundation of continuous innovation in art, technology and culture," reads the introduction to *China Pulse*. "Today, photographic art has expanded to encompass a broader range of technological methods and conceptual

3

interpretations… The central query within photographic art has transitioned from 'what photography should be' to 'what else photography can be'."

The Jimei × Arles Curatorial Award for Photography and Moving Image selection illustrates something of this potential, picking out five proposals by emerging curators selected from an open call. The finalists will receive mentorship and training, and one exhibition will go on to be shown at Three Shadows in Beijing plus other Chinese venues. The proposals include *Bodies of Information* by curators Gwendoline Cho-ning Kam and Li Suchao, a look at media in the algorithmic era and how bodies of information can connect and interact with the human body, and *Beyond the View* by curator Wang Jiayi, which considers how social media morphs real-life experiences and emotions into materials for editing. *Song for the Luddites*, curated by Feng Junyuan, considers the oscillation between irrational fear of technology and labour resistance in the contemporary digital landscape.

Launched in collaboration with Chanel in 2021, the Jimei × Arles Curatorial Award aims to encourage both emerging curators and curatorial practice in general in China. "In the western world, being a curator is a well-known and respected profession, but in China, the curator industry is relatively young, and not everyone is familiar with it," RongRong explains. "Young people who aspire to enter this industry often lack the necessary paths and platforms. This award provides significant support to curators, including financial rewards, funding for exhibition implementation, international research trips, and masterclasses conducted by renowned international curators for other participants."

Chanel is supporting another exhibition at Jimei × Arles: *Clumsily Burgeoning* by actress Huang Xiangli, which presents Polaroids from an unknown woman alongside her own photography. It is part of the *Crossover Photography* section devoted to multimedia shows, which also includes work by sculptor Jiang Sheng, and film

photographer and director Yu Likwai [1]. Sheng's works reflect on the relationship between humans and nature, while Likwai's *Already it is dusk* exhibition, curated by Hai Jei, creates a dream realm for lost souls with photographs and gifs drawn from film productions. The *Greetings from Asia* section, meanwhile, highlights photography from a wider region, and this year is organised by the Singaporean curator Gwen Lee (who is also on the Jimei × Arles committee). Titled *Archipelago: Paradise Revisit*, it showcases artists from the Philippines, Malaysia, Singapore, Thailand and Cambodia, including Elizabeth Gabrielle Lee, Lim Sokchanlina, Wawi Navarroza and Miti Ruangkritya [5].

Jimei × Arles is supported by Jimei District Committee of the Communist Party China, the French Embassy, and ticket sales, but it also needs to attract sponsorships, such as with Chanel, local banks and Vivo Communication Technology. Headquartered in Dongguan, Guangdong, Vivo was founded in 2009 and is now one of the biggest mobile phone manufacturers in

5   *A Convenient Sunset*, 2019
     © Miti Ruangkritya.

6   *Imaginary Museum VII (Picabia)*,
     National Science Center, New Delhi,
     2017, from the series *The Ajaib Ghar*
     Archive © Philippe Calia.

7   *People line up at the docks*, 1908.
     Collection of Liu Gang, courtesy of
     Liu Gang.

the world; it is sponsoring an exhibition at the festival titled *vivo VISION+*. Curated by RongRong, it includes image-makers such as Alex Webb and Francesco Golam, and reflects on the shift in aesthetics and perceptions fostered by smartphones, which have simultaneously spread photography and made it easy to take bursts of images.

"Technological advancements, especially the development of smartphones, have significantly transformed the art of photography in just a few short decades and have also changed our way of life," comments RongRong. "In the past, not everyone had a camera, and people had to visit a photography studio to have their family portraits taken. Later on, almost every household had film or digital cameras.

"Now, with the advent of smartphones, and particularly the advanced development of smartphones in China, they have provided preset photo effects for regular users and professional settings for photographer users. Especially with the widespread popularity of social media, it has become very convenient to take photos and share them on platforms such as WeChat Moments or Instagram. For example, before having a meal, people may take a quick snapshot of their food to share. I believe this has subtly changed our relationship with images. In this era, photography is intimately connected with everyone."

"The art of photography is constantly changing and requires embracing diverse technologies," RongRong adds, although clarifying that this does not equate to abandoning analogue methods. "I believe that if young artists only know how to use smart devices and are unfamiliar with the principles of photography, without stepping into a darkroom, we will gradually lose the history of photography and our understanding of it. This year, we have an exhibition featuring the works of Taiwanese artist

Chen Tsun-shing [3] (titled *Color*, it is the third part of his *Personal Psycho History Trilogy*). His photographs from the 1980s will allow young people to once again see the charm of colour film photography."

Art of collecting

Jimei × Arles also has another exhibition of vintage prints, in its regular *Collector's Tale* exhibition. This show highlights a different collector every year, this time presenting Liu Gang [7] and a photographic album he holds. Made "during the late Qing Dynasty", in 1908, it documents the American Great White Fleet visiting Xiamen, cementing the city's position as one of China's modern treaty ports – a key historical event. "It is a unique collection, and upon seeing it, I decided to invite it for display at Jimei × Arles," says RongRong.

Establishing photography as a collectible art form is one of the reasons RongRong co-founded Jimei × Arles – and, before that, the Three Shadows Photography Art Centre in Beijing. Photography is a young art form in China and its community is still growing, he points out; Three Shadows was the first photography institution in

China when RongRong set it up in 2007 with his partner, Japanese artist inri. They had been inspired by an earlier artists' residency in Vienna, on which RongRong first realised how differently photography was regarded in the west. "The impact and contrast I experienced were immense," he says. "I was shocked by the level of importance photography held in Europe and the general public's awareness of it. Even small photography museums had photography collections.

"The concept of 'art districts' in China gradually took shape after 2000," he continues. "Despite their development, photography as an art form in China still lacked an independent space. At that time, both the authorities and the public did not pay much attention. There were no photography spaces, libraries, residencies, and there were few critics and collectors. An entire photography ecosystem had not been established."

Photography is associated with 'taking' pictures, he says, but he decided he had an opportunity to give back, setting up Three Shadows and helping establish lens-based art in China. Others gradually joined and, over the last five years or so, more initiatives

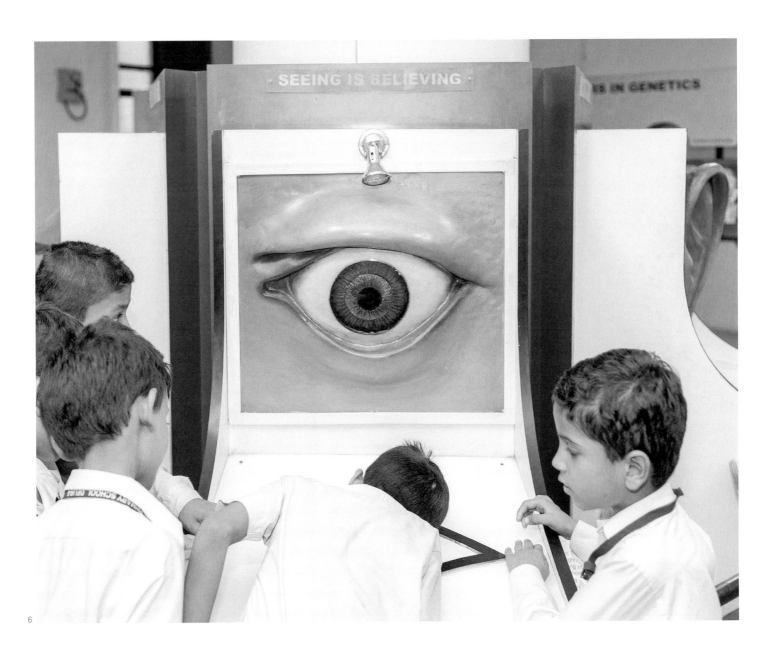

have emerged. RongRong is encouraged by the progress but says there is more to be done. "These organisations are focused on photography of different generations and have been developing their own collections in various cities," he says. "This is a positive phenomenon, but it is not enough. I hope that in the future, there will be dozens of institutions.

"Photography has changed our way of life. The art is still young, but it is vibrant and constantly evolving. With the progress of photography in China, I hope there will be national-level museums and well-established collections in the future. Of course, I can also keenly feel the development of the photography industry in China. There is still a long way to go, but I believe that the future of Chinese photography is promising." **BJP**

@threeshadows_official

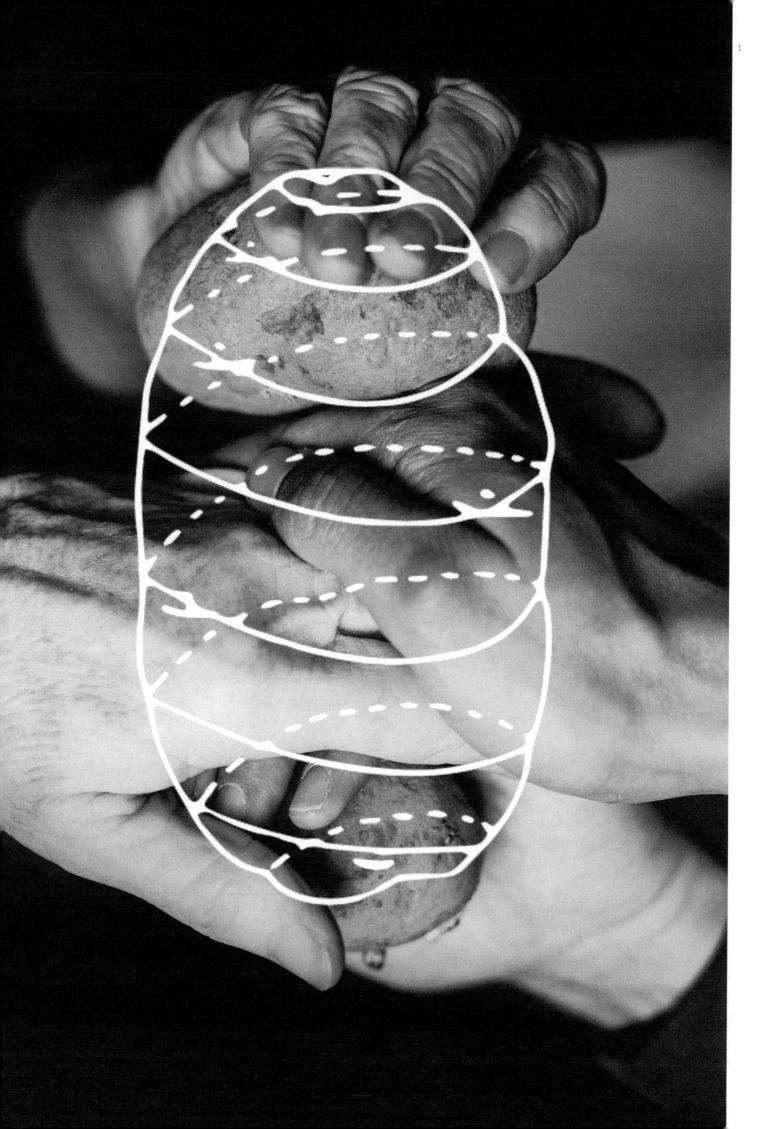

Presented by non-westerners for the first time, the German biennale questions established narratives in photography. Diane Smyth speaks with its three Bangladeshi curators

Biennale für aktuelle Fotografie

1   *Soil Layers*, from the series *Cooking Potato Stories*, 2022 © Ana Núñez Rodriguez.

2   From the series *Of River and Lost Lands, Bangladesh*, 2011–2023 © Sarker Protick. Courtesy of the artist/Shrine Empire Gallery, Delhi.

"What does it mean to listen to images in the context of a biennale? Can we encounter photographs differently, engage with people and their positions distinctively, listen to each other? Crises define our present, shaping and affecting us in uneven ways: ecological catastrophes, political upheaval and economic turmoil all bring about migration and displacement, while states continue to fortify their borders. The consequent pain, oppression and transformation must be confronted collectively and individually, publicly and privately."

So reads the curatorial statement for the 2024 Biennale für aktuelle Fotografie, which opens in March across Mannheim, Ludwigshafen and Heidelberg, three cities in Germany's Rhine-Neckar region. Themed 'Listening to Disquiet', this edition "encourages us to listen, and thus to encounter each other, with empathy,"

the text continues, and for the first time it has been put together by non-western curators: namely Shahidul Alam, Tanzim Wahab and Munem Wasif.

All three hail from Bangladesh and previously worked together at the Chobi Mela International Festival of Photography, founded by Alam (in addition to the Drik Picture Library and Pathshala South Asian Media Institute). Wahab is director of Chobi Mela, as well as the current co-editor of MoMA's *Primary Documents* anthology series on international art. Wasif is co-curator of Chobi Mela, and a photographer who has exhibited at Centre Pompidou, Fotomuseum Winterthur, London's Whitechapel Gallery and others.

Different sections

The curators have divided the biennale into five sections, each considering an aspect of listening and rethinking via photography: *Disruptions of Silence, Inaudible Shifts, Resonances of Loss, Jugolbondi (Duologue)* and *Interferences*. *Disruptions of Silence* takes place in Zephyr photo museum in Mannheim, and collects works that "seek to disrupt the profound silence that societies tolerate". It features photojournalism and fine art photography, including Philip Blenkinsop's documentary images on Burma, and Pakistani visual artist Bani Abidi's *The Reassuring Hand Gestures of Big Men, Small Men, All Men* [3].

Inaudible Shifts takes place in the Wilhelm-Hack-Museum and Kunstverein Ludwigshafen, and considers our relationship with the environment, including how Indigenous knowledge intersects with colonial domination. It features Bangladeshi photographer Sarker Protick's *Of River and Lost Lands* [2], a survey of the River Padma (Ganges) and Singaporean artist Robert Zhao Renhui's *A Guide to the Flora and Fauna*, which shows how the natural world has adapted to human intervention. This section also includes *Cooking Potato Stories* by Ana Núñez Rodríguez [1],

2

3   From the series *The Reassuring Hand Gestures of Big Men, Small Men, All Men*, 2021 © Bani Abidi. Courtesy of Experimenter Gallery, Kolkata, India.

4   *Pictures of Women Working*, 2016 © Carmen Winant. Courtesy of the artist and Patron Gallery.

3

a look at the construction of national identity by an artist based in both Spain and Colombia.

Resonances of Loss takes place at Port25 – Raum für Gegenwartskunst, and challenges historical narratives imposed by those in power, particularly via personal stories. Londoner Naeem Mohaiemen's *Jole Dobe Na (Those Who Do Not Drown)* follows a widower wandering through an abandoned hospital, for example, and considers both modes of care and the afterlife of those who give that care.

The fourth section *Jugolbondi (Duologue)* takes place in the Kunsthalle Mannheim, and is named after a traditional approach to jamming in Indian classical music, in which two soloists, often a vocalist and an instrumentalist, create interdependent harmonies. It includes series by duos Camille Lévêque and Lucie Khahoutian, a French-Armenian pairing; and Ritu Sarin and Tenzing Sonam [5], who have heritage from India and Tibet. Sarin and Sonam are showing *Shadow Circus*, "a personal archive of Tibetan resistance" which weaves together photographs, letters, maps and video installations.

Interferences at Heidelberger Kunstverein deals with public engagement, asking how exhibitions can develop as spaces of creative exchange rather than extraction. It includes work Patrick Waterhouse developed in collaboration with the Aboriginal community based at Australia's Warlukurlangu Art Centre, and Carmen Winant's series *Pictures of Women Working* [4], an image collage which questions what constitutes female labour by showing women beautifying, nursing children, having sex, protesting, practising self-defence, and making art.

"One of the things that was very important for us is diversity," Alam says. "We've tried to question how the representation of what we call 'majority world countries' has largely been done

4

5   From the series *Shadow Circus*, 2019–ongoing © Ritu Sarin & Tenzing Sonam. Courtesy of Lhamo Tsering Archive/White Crane Films.

5

For Alam, the gaze underpins all these concerns – the power relationships involved and how they might be subverted. Listening is not just a physical act, he says, but a philosophical problem of "how to subvert the traditional role that photographers have inhabited as hunter-gatherers, how we want to be able to listen to the photographs, and how the photographs speak to us." And while this speaks to current concerns in photography – Alam's words echo Tina M Campt's influential 2017 publication, *Listening to Images* – it is also an area that has long preoccupied the trio.

Alam was motivated by challenging the stereotypical representation of culture, and questioning who tells the story, when he founded the influential Drik in 1989; interrogating his own position was part of the mission. One of Drik's early moves was to build a women's photo collective, while Chobi Mela has worked with non-traditional photography spaces to build up an audience "which is not the typical gallery audience". He and the other curators have also reached out to similar organisations in the Global South to build up closer connections, such as Johannesburg's Market Photo Workshop.

"It's really how these different places are going to collaborate, how we can create a network and a larger dialogue to get to know each other, and see what we can do together," Wasif says. "This can be a start and an interference, and that's exciting." **BJP**

by white western photographers. Europe is the birthplace of photography, and has a great tradition of photography, and there's a substantial amount of work [in the biennale] from Europe. But photography has a problematic history, in its association with colonialism, and it's also a very male space.

"So we have created a very eclectic, diverse group, and we have also looked at how the European identity is not so clearly cut and dried," he continues. "Many of the artists now based in Europe [in the biennale] have multiple identities, and we have tried to embrace that complexity."

Structural shifts
Alam, Wahab and Wasif – "three bearded men," as Alam puts it – have also invited three women curators to advise on the project: Yasmine Eid-Sabbagh, N'Goné Fall and Tanvi Mishra. Eid-Sabbagh is a member of the Arab Image Foundation whose work includes a collaboration with inhabitants of Burj al-Shamali, a Palestinian refugee camp. Senegalese curator and editor Fall is one-time editorial director of *Revue Noire*, and has previously curated the Bamako and Dakar Biennales. Mishra, who is based in New Delhi, was creative director of *The Caravan*, and curated the Discovery

Award at the 2023 Les Rencontres d'Arles. "We needed to question our own perspective and ensure we didn't get caught up in our blind spots," Alam says. "We're working together to try to shake things up."

"We have always worked in a collaborative format, so we are also doing this in Germany," Wasif adds. "We like to have some of our colleagues and friends on board, so that they can bring different kinds of knowledge. We have a different kind of curatorial and institutional practice in Bangladesh, so we know for sure that we have our limitations. These three voices [Eid-Sabbagh, Fall and Mishra] bring in different kinds of reading and perspective."

Alam, Wahab and Wasif have also considered the diversity of their audience in Germany, saying they were surprised how few of Mannheim's sizeable migrant community visit museums. White-cube galleries can feel intimidating, they point out, so while they are happy "to utilise these beautiful spaces", they also want to create something welcoming, Alam explains. "We are also thinking how we might be able to create bridges between these spaces and the local community: how we might use the openings, offering food and other elements."

On show
Biennale für aktuelle Fotografie 2024 takes place at various venues across Rhine-Neckar, Germany, from 09 March to 19 May 2024. biennalefotografie.de/en

1

Mixing his signature celebrity portraits with intimate images of his own family, Micaiah Carter's new book creates a space that celebrates unparalleled beauty in everyone

Words by Diane Smyth

2

All the beauty

Born in 1995 in Victorville, California, Micaiah Carter got into photography via magazines, Tumblr, Beyoncé videos and family photos. He worked for a spell on a local newspaper then won a scholarship to Parsons School of Design in New York, and has had a meteoric rise to fame. Now based back in California, he shoots for clients such as *Vanity Fair*, *Vogue*, *The New York Times*, Nike, Ralph Lauren and Lancôme, and has worked with a who's who of contemporary American culture, including Pharrell, Zendaya, Ben Affleck and The Weeknd.

Even so, his portraits seem intimate, warm in colour and vibe. His career is glamorous, but his photographs avoid hard-edged glamour; he works with powerful players, but his portraits exude gentleness. So it is perhaps not surprising to see that his monograph, *What's My Name*, includes images of his relatives and vintage shots from his family album alongside fashion photography and celebrity portraiture. Perhaps what is more remarkable is that, to Carter, there is not so much difference between them. Some photographers fiercely divide their personal and professional work, but that is not his style.

"I used to love to go through the family albums as a kid," he says. "I'm the youngest in my family, so a lot of my relatives had passed away, but to have a way of knowing who they were, of knowing their style, their smile, their eyes, understanding why they were placed in that part of the book, it was all super important to me. My grandmother used to always sit on the front porch too, and go through the family album and offer oral history, which I thought was amazing.

"But I feel like it's the same for me, that the way I look at Pharrell is the same way I look at my great-uncle in a photo," he adds. "Not knowing him, but hearing stories about him and being excited about it, especially because the people that I photograph have all inspired me in one way or another."

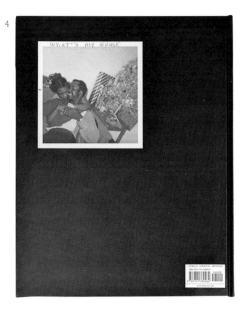

Carter's father was in the air force and was involved in the civil rights movement and the Black Panthers, "able to express himself in the Black is Beautiful movement", says Carter. Maybe he passed on a sense that everyone has something special because that is what Carter reaches for in his shoots. As his friend and collaborator Tracee Ellis Ross puts it in the introduction to *What's My Name*: "He creates a space that is less of a set and more of an exchange; kind of like hanging with a friend in their backyard on a sunny day in that peace that comes after all the food has been eaten, the catching up is finished, and you are just there together without an agenda. This is what he captures – the safety of connection, the beauty of being."

"You're just able to be your full self, and not feel ashamed of being a little weird or a little different," says Carter. "Embracing that is really beautiful. That's the best, and the most original. If you're trying to emulate someone else it can feel a little forced. Honesty makes a good portrait – that moment where they're confident in themselves, when there's trust involved. Creating an environment that is relaxed and that has nuances of love creates a great portrait."

Carter's father died in 2021 and the photographer responded with his first solo show, *American Black Beauty*, at SN37 Gallery New York, in which he also mixed his own photographs of relatives, family photographs, and professional work. With his book, Carter is keen to continue this trajectory, working on self-assigned projects alongside commissions. He is drawn towards photographing his nieces, he says, towards the feeling of doing the shoot as much as the images.

"I often don't share the images, it's my family and I'm protective over them," he says. "But to see my nieces laugh and smile – to be a little nervous but then, at the end of the session, feel good about themselves because they're like 'Wow, I actually am valued' – I gravitate towards it. But it's not just from them. It's honestly everyone that I love to photograph." **BJP**

micaiahcarter.com

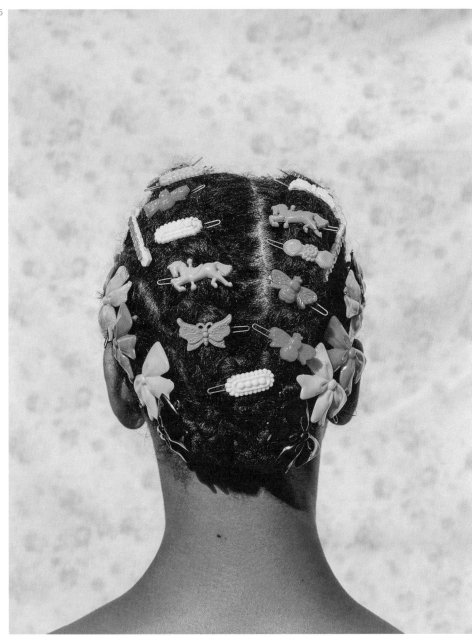

In print

Micaiah Carter: What's My Name is published by Prestel Publishing, priced £45.
prestelpublishing.penguinrandomhouse.de

Any Answers
Sabina Jaskot-Gill

Interview by Philippa Kelly
Portrait by David Parry

Following a three-year remodel and a renewed presentation of its collection, the National Portrait Gallery (NPG) opened its doors to the public once again in June 2023. Heading up its photography team is Sabina Jaskot-Gill, who was appointed senior curator at the same time. Prior to joining the gallery in 2016, Jaskot-Gill spent time working for photographer Karen Knorr, completed a PhD exploring Polish postwar photography and lectured in photographic history and theory at Sotheby's Institute of Art in London. Here, she discusses her career, her hopes for the NPG's photography collection, and the Taylor Wessing Photo Portrait Prize, which is on show at the gallery until 25 February 2024.

Francesca Woodman piqued my interest in photography as a medium, so it will be a nice full-circle moment when the NPG exhibits her work next spring. I discovered her work while studying art history and English literature at the University of Edinburgh and, off the back of my degree, tried to learn more about the history of photography. I took a master's degree in photography at Sotheby's Institute, which was led by the brilliant Juliet Hacking. She became one in a line of impressive women that I studied or worked with who have mentored and inspired me throughout my career.

When I was growing up in Bradford – quite a long way from the National Portrait Gallery – I often visited a place called Salts Mill to look at the work of David Hockney. It was such a transformative thing as a child, to go to a gallery and experience art. And obviously that set me on the path to where I am today. So it's really important for me in my role at the NPG to be working with the gallery's Learning team to develop our activities around photography for young people. It's about bringing the next generation into the gallery and finding something that inspires them.

Across the three years that the NPG has been closed, everyone kept saying, 'What have you been up to? It's been so quiet'. But it's actually been incredibly busy. One thing we've been doing is working with local community groups, to try to identify sitters from their communities who deserve to be represented in a national collection. We've got over 250,000 photographic objects but we're a living, working collection, and we're continuing to acquire and commission new work. We want to make sure that we're representing the people who are contributing to British culture today.

Our acquisition process is slightly different to other museums – we're very much driven by the sitter rather than the artist. The first questions we ask are always 'Who is the sitter? How have they contributed to British society and culture?'. The artist is almost secondary, which is not to say that they're not important, but that we're a social history museum as well as an art gallery. We can tell stories in ways that other museums can't.

The representation of women within the gallery's collection is something that we've been working on since I joined the NPG over seven years ago. I think all of that work has come to fruition – and will continue to do so. At the moment, in our post-1900 galleries, the representation of women on the walls is 48 per cent. And that is continuing – I'm currently working on a series of acquisitions from young, emerging women photographers that we hope to display in the near future.

In the earliest years that I worked on the Taylor Wessing Photo Portrait Prize there was more experimentation with techniques. We used to get a lot of cyanotypes, Polaroids or tintypes, whereas now there seems to be less experimentation with the type of media, but more experimentation in terms of composition. This year's selection feels more introspective. I don't know if that's because of the pandemic and how our lives have changed as a result, but there does seem to be a focus on family and looking inwards into one's own life.

There's definitely more diversity in terms of the artists and sitters that are featured, and in terms of the styles of portraiture. We used to get a lot of editorial work, and we still do, but I've noticed a shift towards artists increasingly using the prize to showcase their personal projects. I think that shows how the prize is evolving and really embracing the voices in contemporary photography today. **BJP**

npg.org.uk

Our featured Projects include
Ada Marino taking inspiration from her
grandmother, while Nikita Teryoshin's
images of arms fairs are more urgent
than ever. Adib Chowdhury looks
to a Sufi saint to explore modern
Bangladesh, and Tara Laure Claire
tours portrait studios to reframe India.
Plus works by Ollie Adegboye, Pauline
Rowan and Rica May Tumanguil

Projects

Words by Diane Smyth

Born in the UK to Bangladeshi parents, Adib Chowdhury studied political science at the London School of Economics and started working as a photographer in 2015, covering issues around armed conflict, human rights and environmental stories for organisations such as *The Guardian*, Agence France-Presse and Al Jazeera Plus.

From 2018, he was based in Lebanon and covering the Middle East. However, when Covid hit, he returned to the UK and found himself back in his childhood room, reflecting on his archive and the stories he was told in his youth. In particular, he thought of tales about Shah Jalal, a 13th-century Sufi saint who was handed a prophecy that made him a famous scholar, military leader and religious figure. This narrative had always been – and is in many cases for children of diaspora – a link to the motherland and, in the midst of lockdown, planted the idea to turn the legend into a photographic body of work.

Shah Jalal's story is that of a high-class Sufi child, born either in modern-day Turkey or Yemen (there are conflicting historical records), who became a famous Sufi scholar at a young age. One day, his uncle handed him a glass vial and told him of the vision he had for him: to spread Islam until the colour of the soil in the vial matched that of the earth beneath his feet. Shah Jalal's story then covers an epic, decade-long journey across the Middle East which ends in the Bangladeshi region of Sylhet, where Chowdhury's parents are originally from. "You can't visit Sylhet without someone mentioning Shah Jalal or his dargah [burial place and shrine]," Chowdhury explains. "It's integral to the history and culture of the region."

As Covid receded, Chowdhury went to visit the shrine and decided to trace Shah Jalal's journey

Adib Chowdhury

back through Bangladesh and India. Chowdhury made images as he travelled, loosely guided by the traditional stories, but also feeling his way. It was very different to photojournalism. "It was liberating," he explains. "I'm used to working with an assignment in mind, within certain parameters and contexts, but this was so free-flowing. I wrote down some themes that appear in the story, such as 'love' or 'exile', and I mapped out certain locations, but aside from that, I wanted to turn up and see what unfolded. I thought, 'Let's just let the pieces fall into place – the story is so imbued with the culture that these symbols will surely surface'.

"I would sit there with my camera on my tripod and wait for certain scenes, or I'd be driving and suddenly see something perfect," he adds. "It was my first project shooting on film, and I didn't get anything developed along the way. I wanted it to be intuitive, using my natural curiosity to feel a scene. It felt meditative and slow, there was no sense of rush at all."

Chowdhury named the series *Lal Mati* (*Red Soil*) and some of the images pick out this feature; others focus on the rivers and deltas that criss-cross Bangladesh. Some hone in on ravens, which are important characters in Shah Jalal's story as they cause trouble and act as informers. One image shows an elderly man, who evoked for Chowdhury the old saint, while several simply pick up on a mood.

Chowdhury also freely mixed locations, pointing out that folklore does the same because Shah Jalal long predates the creation of modern-day Bangladesh, or even India. At a time of increasing nationalism within both countries, narratives such as this point to a time before the modern-day national entities existed, as well as Chowdhury's own family history; his father has an old East Pakistan passport, he says, as at one time that was his country. Chowdhury adds that he is called 'Bidesi' in Sylhet, which means 'foreigner' and is often applied to those raised in Britain.

"The vast majority of the Bangladeshi community in the UK has origins in Sylhet," he explains. "After the Second World War there was a huge need for textile workers in Britain, and people from Sylhet had that expertise, as well as links to working with the British as seafarers, and so viewed England as a place they had some connection to."

This thought feeds into wider work Chowdhury is making about Bangladesh, investigating globalisation and how it has affected the country. "I'm looking at capitalism and how Bangladesh has been used like a factory, or a resource, where even the people themselves have become commodities," he says, referring to an ongoing project on the lives of migrant workers in the Middle East. "Back in the late 1990s/early 2000s, everyone was talking about globalisation but now you don't hear that word so much. Are we as Bangladeshis or the developing world better for it? Or is it just a form of neocolonialism? Who has it really benefitted?" **BJP**

adibphotography.com

In the introduction to her 2005 book *On Female Body Experience*, the theorist Iris Marion Young asks: "How do girls and women constitute their experienced world through their movement and orientation in places? What are some of the feelings of ambivalence, pleasure, power, shame, objectification, and solidarity that women have about bodies, their shape, flows, and capacities?" In the following chapters, Young explores what it is to exist in a woman's body, to navigate the restricted spaces assigned to women by patriarchal societies.

Young's queries hold great significance for Ada Marino, whose project *New Moons* tackles similar themes with an equal sense of purpose. The work simultaneously laments the restrictive nature of gender norms and abortion laws while acting as a call for their end. It is filled with narratives of resistance and perseverance that, for Marino, are born from highly personal experiences.

"My work is strongly influenced by the experiences of my grandmother, who was physically and verbally abused, which consequently had repercussions on my entire family," the photographer explains. "My artistic formation is deeply rooted in my southern Italian culture and family experiences, mirroring the patriarchal domination that has surrounded me since childhood." Marino's goal is to use this lived experience to create connections, building bridges between her own struggles and those of women the world over.

She began this work with 2022's *Paterfamilias*, an autobiographical project that delved into the story of her grandmother, who "was beaten and denigrated by an authoritarian husband," she describes. Marino says the project represents her "daunting past", and the visual investigation explores the oppression of women in the domestic sphere, including the sense of conflict and oppression created by unsafe shelter. Her latest series offers a natural progression in theme, moving

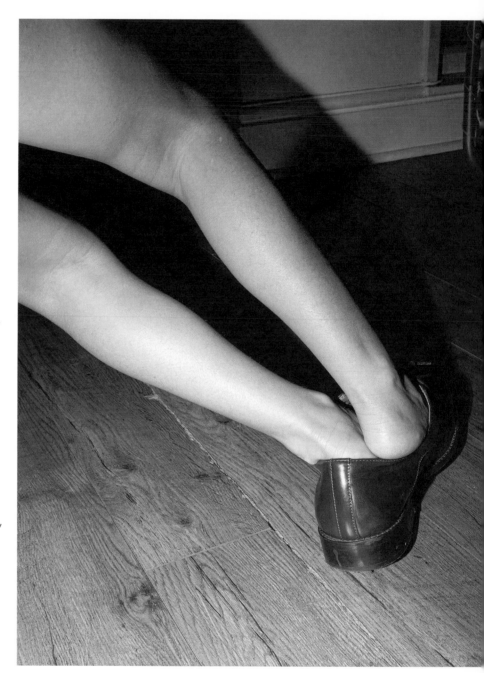

Ada Marino

from her past to her aspirations for the future, and adopting a more chilling photographic approach. *New Moons* conjures a stronger sense of the supernatural than the previous work, including images that are eerie, almost ghostly, and weaving moments of girlhood with religious iconography to create a visual language akin to a Hollywood exorcism. These qualities are not incidental. Marino's images represent different and fluctuating emotional states, she says, echoing writer Betty Friedan's "problem that has no name" – the elusive, invisible and intangible feminine mystique.

But in spite of the complex and sometimes painful subject matter, *New Moons* offers a message of hope. The title's plural nods to the many ways in which womanhood can be experienced, encouraging solidarity across communities. The lunar phase from which the project takes its name also symbolises the closing of one cycle and the beginning of another, suggesting a new state of being for all.

Marino hopes that the series can help people begin this new cycle, to find the courage to dismantle oppressive structures, and the strength to replace them with an egalitarian future. She describes the work as an incitement to social education, a medium through which she encourages viewers to learn more about the impact of male hegemony on women. Finally, she says, it is a reminder that in order to successfully fight against gender discrimination, all women must be united.

"*New Moons* is my beacon of light for anyone who has felt the weight of oppression," Marino says. "It does not want to be a dormant hope, but expresses a certainty of redemption that occurs through the awakening of societal consciences on women's conditions." **BJP**

adamarino.com

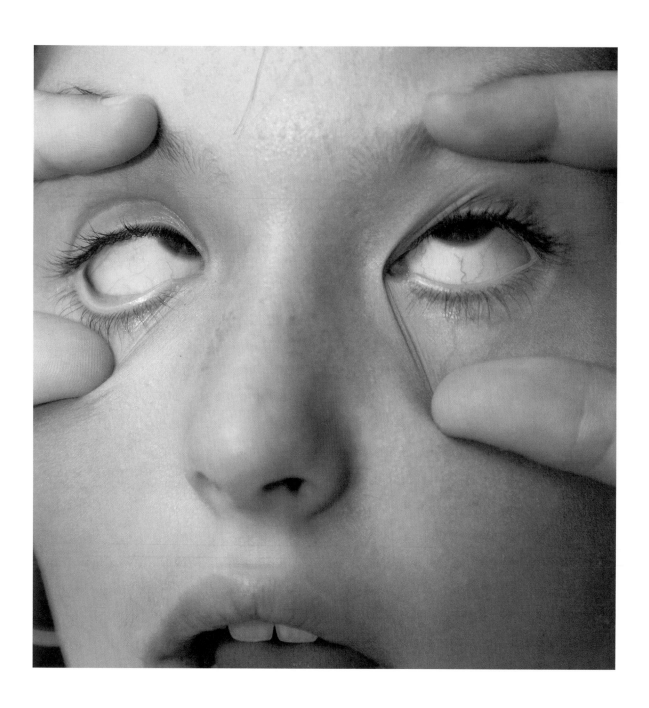

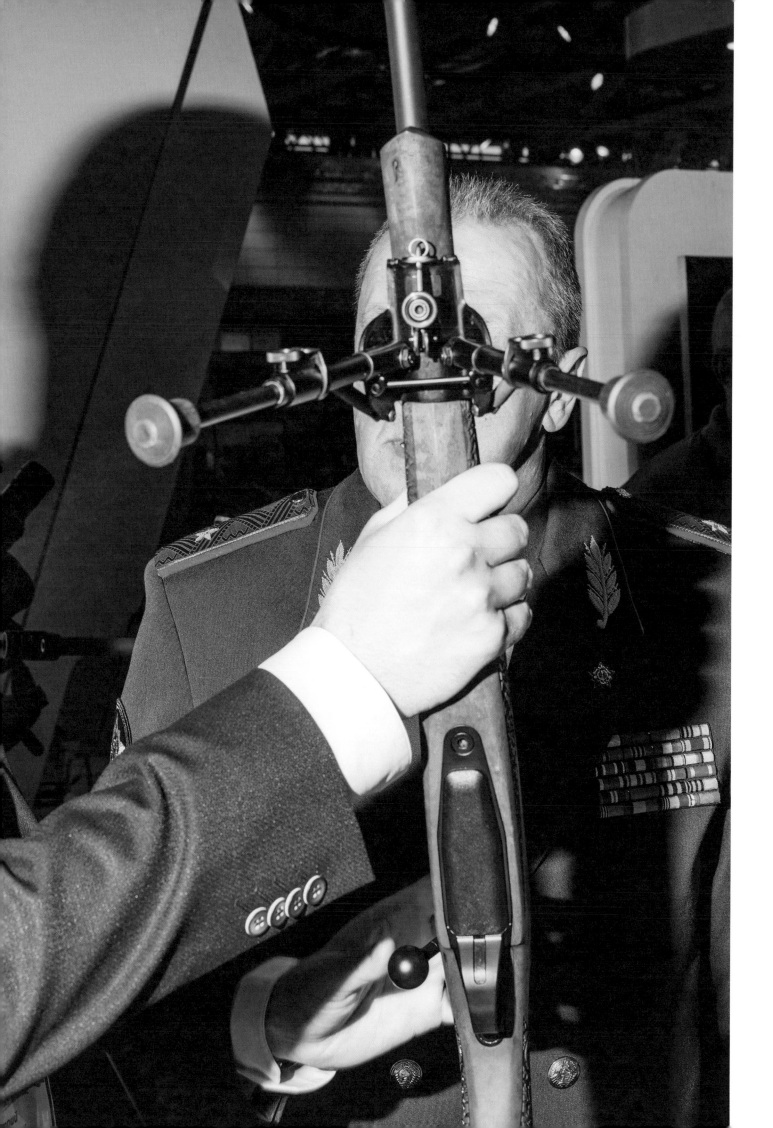

Words by Ravi Ghosh

In a conflict-ridden world, weapons are instruments of both war and politics. In October 2023, the Swedish defence ministry offered its Gripen fighter jets to a western coalition that was considering sending planes to Ukraine, on the condition that Sweden be admitted to Nato. Turkey's President Erdoğan had previously used his veto over Sweden's membership, before dropping it in July. He is currently adding new conditions to the talks, indicating he would support Swedish membership once F-16 jets are passed from the US to Turkey.

Before all this, weapons have to be designed, licensed, manufactured and sold – ostensibly to legitimate actors, but also to proxy wars, militias and paramilitaries. Much of the window shopping happens at arms fairs, which Russian-born photographer Nikita Teryoshin has been photographing since 2016. His first visit was to the International Defence Industry Exhibition (MSPO) in Kielce, Poland, while he was still a student at the University of Applied Sciences & Arts in Dortmund. He was met with a reception for military helicopters held by Airbus – champagne and finger food next to killing machines.

"I was thinking, 'Wow, it's like the opposite of war – great weather, people are super polite, you get food and drink for free'," he recalls. Teryoshin has since travelled to at least 17 fairs for *Nothing Personal*, a series of cold, flash-heavy images in which the weapons command more attention than people. The project will be published as a book by Gost in February 2024. Teryoshin decided not to photograph anyone's face. "The way I show this business is through metaphor, because it's a shadowy business," he says. It is an outsider's view, but also "a comment, an essay", a provocation for viewers to research the industry. "Mixing capitalism and stock markets with the arms trade is one of the worst things that can happen," he says ruefully.

In 2020, the estimated value of the global arms trade was $112billion, but the conflicts in Ukraine and Israel-Gaza have bolstered sales; German manufacturer Rheinmetall's share price more than doubled in the two months following the Russian invasion into Ukraine. The UK's arms exports doubled during 2022 to a record £8.5billion, with Qatar the biggest buyer. *Nothing Personal* shows the full breadth of the equipment behind these numbers. Tanks, armoured suits, rifles and intelligence devices are shown in prototype or unused form, with an unnerving sterility which matches the attendees' tailored suits.

Most of all, Teryoshin is attuned to the ways the industry justifies itself – a combination of wilful ignorance, profit-chasing and close ties to the security architecture of superpowers such as the US, China and India. By holding these narratives alongside the realities of today's wars, dark ironies emerge. Slogans are a straightforward example: Kalashnikov Concern rebranded in 2014 under the slogan 'Protecting Peace'; ITT Inc uses the line 'Engineered for Life'. *Nothing Personal* is about conveying these ironies, exposing not just these closed fairs, but the implications of a world in which militarisation is incentivised. A huge battlefield-inspired cake at the UAE's Navdex fair in 2019 is the most absurd example of these juxtapositions, while red carpets, copious wine and ornate bouquets feature across the series.

"For people working there, it doesn't actually matter what they're selling," Teryoshin says. "You can sell vacuum cleaners, cars, killing machines, as long as you maintain the idea that what you're doing is good because it's for security, fighting against 'bad guys'." An earlier project, *Hornless Heritage*, saw him go behind the scenes in Germany's dairy industry, where cows are genomically selected and artificially inseminated. Teryoshin sees similarities with the arms fairs in terms of ethical triangulation – millions of people eat meat despite knowing about the extractive and abusive nature of factory farming, and people continue to develop and sell weapons while civilians and soldiers are killed. "These ironies are coming not just from my point of view, this world is isolated from the public," Teryoshin says. "People are living in a parallel universe." Even so, he picks out the fairs' banality as perhaps their most sinister quality: "For a weapons trader, the best thing is to sell to both sides of the conflict." **BJP**

nikitateryoshin.com

Nikita Teryoshin

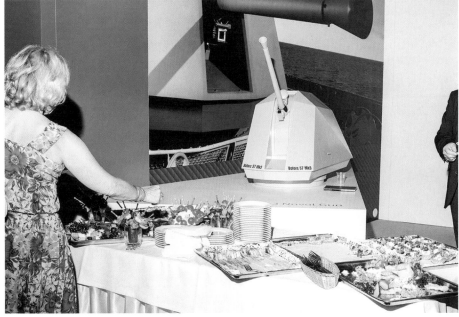

Words by Diane Smyth

Rica May Tumanguil was born and brought up in Tuguegarao, a city in the Philippines. The country was long under colonial rule, occupied first by Spain and then by the US; it gained independence in 1946 but, says Tumanguil, western values persist, including Eurocentric standards of beauty. Lighter skin is seen as desirable for finding a partner, or even establishing a career, and darker skin is sometimes openly mocked. Some Filipinos, especially young women, turn to whitening products in a bid to bleach themselves into conformity.

"As for many, it was a major part of my experience growing up," says Tumanguil. "I was bullied and teased for having a more tanned complexion and, as a teenage girl wanting to be seen as beautiful, I used papaya soap to try to lighten my skin, as did my mother and sister. A common sight at the local market was women with peeling red skin after they had bleached, and it was also common for cheap skin-lightening soaps containing mercury to be sold at the market."

More recently, some skin-lightening commercials have elicited a backlash in the Philippines, Tumanguil adds, but generally these voices are quiet in the wider social discourse. She moved to London in 2015 to live with her father and to study photography at London South Bank University, and for her final project, opted to protest against the beauty practice, making a series ironically titled *The Fairest of Them All*. Taking a series of self-portraits on Polaroids, she applied skin-lightening products directly to the prints, allowing them to strip and damage the surfaces.

Tumanguil chose to work with Polaroids because the melting emulsions she lifted from them felt fleshy; the resulting work expresses the experience of skin-lightening, she says, serving as a literal reminder of just how caustic these products are. The fact that her face disappears in some images also suggests the notion of erasure and the effacement of non-western aesthetics and people. "Through Eurocentric and Orientalist lenses, the Philippines, as with other colonised lands, now face the after-effects of western white supremacy," she comments.

Tumanguil discovered photography through her iPhone, but found herself drawn to analogue while at university. LSBU does not have a darkroom, but she met a friendly community at the Lakeside Darkroom, who gave her guidance she continues to draw on now she has graduated. Her tutors pushed her artistically too, but *The Fairest of Them All* was directly inspired by Stephen Gill, particularly his project *Best Before End*. Taking colour negative films and dunking them in energy drinks, Gill distorted and corrupted his images and, as with skin lightening, damaged his health in the process.

Gill's project is a commentary on rest and a 24-hour society that almost forbids it; Tumanguil's work is about impossible beauty standards and the ongoing impact of colonial and cultural imperialism. "I wanted to create a project that presented the viewer with overwhelming texture," she says, "using processes that can only be achieved through these physical methods." BJP

@_ricalt.mm

Rica May Tumanguil

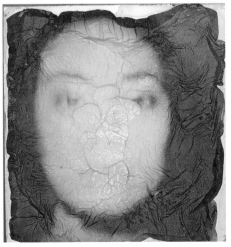

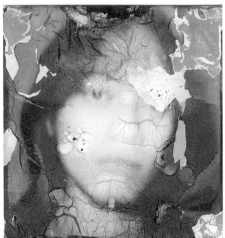

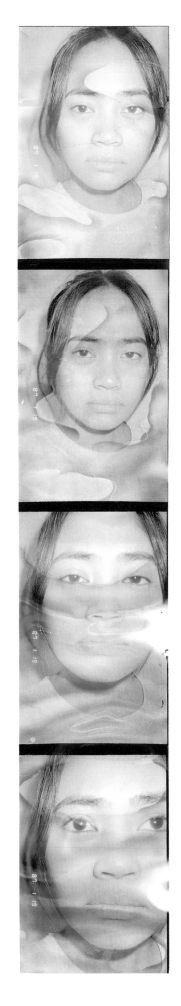

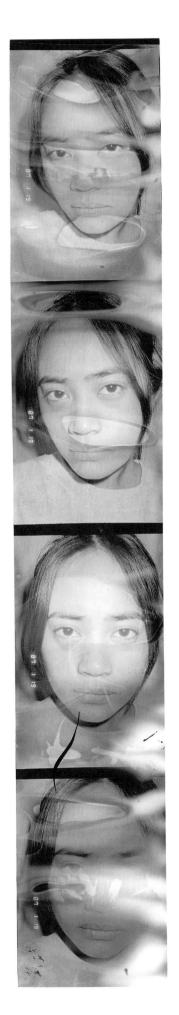

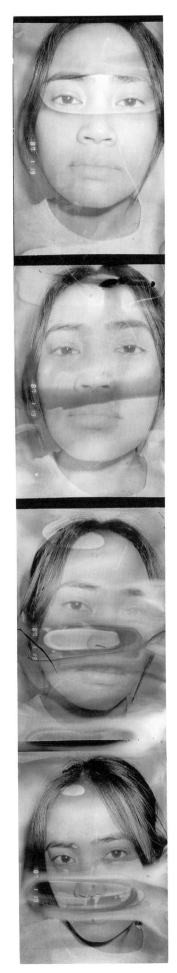

Words by Philippa Kelly

Pauline Rowan was wholly prepared for the realities of motherhood – or so she thought. The 40-year-old had a caring partner, parents who would support her, and a plan for the birth of her child; a natural event during which she aspired to feel at one with the world. When her daughter arrived in April 2018, everything went smoothly.

When the baby was just a few days old, Rowan and her partner moved from Dublin to a new home, an idyllic cottage in the Irish countryside. At the heart of a charming public garden, and just a few minutes drive from her family, it should have been an ideal abode. And yet, exhausted, confused and surrounded by the endless detritus of parenthood, the new mother felt disconnected. "It was the machine of being a mother that I wasn't prepared for," Rowan recalls. "I didn't know when it was going to stop, then I realised that it wasn't." In an attempt to take control of the chaos that surrounded her, Rowan began to take photographs. With her daughter often cradled in her arms, she used the only camera she could: her phone.

Over the next 18 months she made *Between the Gates*, and the images in the series speak clearly to her sense of separation and uncertainty during this time. Fragmented and dreamlike, they are, in some ways, unsettling. "I was alone a lot with my daughter," Rowan remembers. "There's many dark images of me standing at the back door just looking out into the yard, because when I finally had a bit of time to myself, there was nothing, no one there."

Rowan's husband was working long hours, her parents could not visit as often as she had hoped and, just outside her windows, visitors to the public garden surrounding her home peered in. The crowds began to feel like a physical manifestation of her insecurities, seemingly judging her failed attempts to become an ideal mother, wife and woman. "Looking back on the images now, there's very little editing," she says. "I knew that if they looked like a contradiction and didn't quite make sense, then they belonged in the project, and were part of my days or nights of being a mother."

Despite this relaxed approach to editing – mirrored in the many photographs, sometimes presented Polaroid-style, that make up the work – there are shots that stand out to Rowan. A baby's forearm fashioned from wax, dismembered trees, and weeds forcing their way through cracked pavements represent the boundary between the

expected and the achievable. Dead branches hold unclear meaning, while furniture in the midst of being discarded embodies the fragmented elements of a home. Even so, today these images remind Rowan that, through destruction, something new can be made.

Perhaps the most symbolic photographs are those of the magnificent flowers that surrounded Rowan and her partner's home. During the photographer's first months as a mother, an ostensibly joyful time, the reality and chaos of which is often obscured, these explosions of life sat uncomfortably alongside broken flowerpots and grass trampled by visiting children. "I suppose it's a little violent," she reflects. "But I suppose birth is violent too." **BJP**

paulinerowan.com

Pauline Rowan

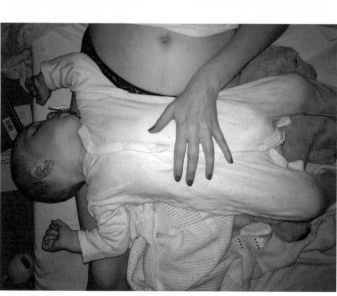

Words by Ravi Ghosh

One evening in August 2020, nine friends got together in Ollie Adegboye's flat in Tottenham, north London. The men had all known each other for 22 years, having met at secondary school on the London-Essex border. They talked about the pandemic, their jobs, money and relationships. Two or three of them already had children, while several others were weeks away from becoming first-time fathers. Adegboye knew his partner was pregnant at the time, but was not ready to announce it yet.

"It was the first time I had ever seen a group of Black men speaking so openly and honestly about fatherhood, about themselves, about their expectations," Adegboye says. He decided to start photographing the men with their children in early 2021. By June 2023, all 10 who had met that evening had become fathers. The portraits have become *Bàbá, Father*, a book and an ongoing project which so far features 63 Black dads with their children. Thirty are Adegboye's friends, others are friends' partners and acquaintances, and a small number he sourced through a casting agency. And while they all have parenthood in common, in reality this factor unifies a huge range of experience. "All have different theories on how to raise a child," Adegboye tells me.

The fathers discussed how their upbringings had informed their parenting styles, which were often influenced by their West Indian or African cultural roots. (Adegboye is of Nigerian origin, hence the Yoruba accents in the work's title). "They're all thinking and feeling similar things about the future – they're quite cautious and wary of how things are going," Adegboye says. Schooling, housing, safety, bullying: all these topics were swirling in the subjects' minds as they held their young children still for the camera. One friend was intent on his child becoming a doctor. Others talked about their fears and anxieties.

When does a father become a Black father? It is a question Adegboye has toyed with and posed to those he photographed. In the first months and years, the men mostly just saw themselves as parents, fulfilling their role without having to consider the outside world. But fathers with older children (teenagers especially) described to Adegboye a racial consciousness mandated by attention from police, discrimination at school, and the wider forces at play for those growing up Black in London today. The absence of text makes these subtleties difficult to detect in the pictures, so *Bàbá, Father* becomes a kind of untethered index – a set of men whose inner lives accumulate to cover a swathe of the Black British experience. The range ensures that hidden facets of fatherhood are also represented. Three of the men have full custody of their daughters, for example, but only Adegboye and the fathers in question know who they are.

"I wanted it to represent these men with their children, at peace," he says. The images are clean and occasionally stylised, a nod to Adegboye's background in commercial portrait photography. He intends to continue the project, focusing perhaps on fathers with uniforms that determine their livelihoods – and therefore their children's (and society's) perception of them – such as firemen or doctors. The cover of the *Bàbá, Father* book features two-year-old Adegboye with his own father, a distant starting point. "It really was just trying to make nice images of these Black men," Adegboye concludes. "I felt I'd never seen a lot of those." **BJP**

ollieadegboye.com

Ollie Adegboye

Words by Ravi Ghosh

Tara Laure Claire has long been intrigued by portrait studios, recognising their importance in Indian photographic history and as sites of self-fashioning for families, couples, colleagues and models eager to project a certain image. Her project *The Studio* pays homage to these spaces while also exploring two personal threads. First, there is Claire's experience shooting fashion editorials and working with stylists and models; second, her desire to produce a joyful series on India, countering depictions of the country she has seen while living in London and Paris. Hers is a vision of a nation made (sometimes literally) using its own mirrors.

"The idea was to bring together all these emotive elements of the studios, and then my personal style took it into a different direction," Claire says. She was inspired by retro studios in Karnataka and other south India states, but *The Studio* was shot entirely in London and gradually departed from its fashion premise towards a fine art self-referentiality, with lamps, mirrors and the edges of decorative sets visible in the images. In the end, she discarded many of the clothes she had initially brought for the shoots. In the final series, a man looks over his shoulder, shirtless as he gently prises open ribbed curtains. In another shot, a couple beam while sitting on a moped in front of a nursery-like mural of flowers and blobby clouds.

Claire etched or painted on several of the prints, echoing the DIY techniques studio owners used for subjects who lacked the means to buy lavish saris and tunics.

The Studio also traces photography's mechanical evolutions, nodding to ambrotypes and tintypes as well as the bright fabric backdrops favoured as when digital cameras became widespread. Claire drew inspiration from prints in Indian family albums and on glass plates, which she found in flea markets in India and Europe. She also referenced imagery from Africa, another big market for portrait studios, and mentions Malick Sidibé and Samuel Fosso. Bollywood hairstyles and poses also found their way into her series, which has a distinctly theatrical air, the models like actors rotating through various roles as if posing for promotional pictures from a multi-act comedy.

Born in France to a Punjabi family, Claire attended boarding school in the Himalayas before studying performance art at Central Saint Martins. After travelling in India to research *The Studio*, she began to critique the western perspective she had absorbed in London and Paris. "When you're in Europe, everybody seems to have their blinders on [when thinking about India]," she says. "They can't see past the chaos – there's this need to dilute things." She wanted to pursue a project that celebrated the country's visual culture and ingenuity, factors rarely recognised beyond its own borders. She also sought to represent everyday people without resorting to poverty porn, and the familiar depictions in which working-class Indians are defined solely by their living conditions.

Claire is planning two other series in this vein, constituting what she terms a chapter-by-chapter survey of India's "dying arts and artistry". The next body of work will document magicians in the country, whose tricks are often dumbed down when emulated in the west. After that she plans to follow the country's dwindling equestrian scene, tracing regional nobles and breeding practices which stretch back centuries.

The Studio is about positivity through complexity, about layers of references that move beyond the equation of an Indian model or "brown face" as adequate representation for a vast, heterogeneous country. There remains a postcolonial hangover in the diaspora, Claire says. "In the west, you're taught to deny yourself and deny India. It's my duty to make a body of work romanticising it." **BJP**

taralaureclaire.studio

Tara Laure Claire

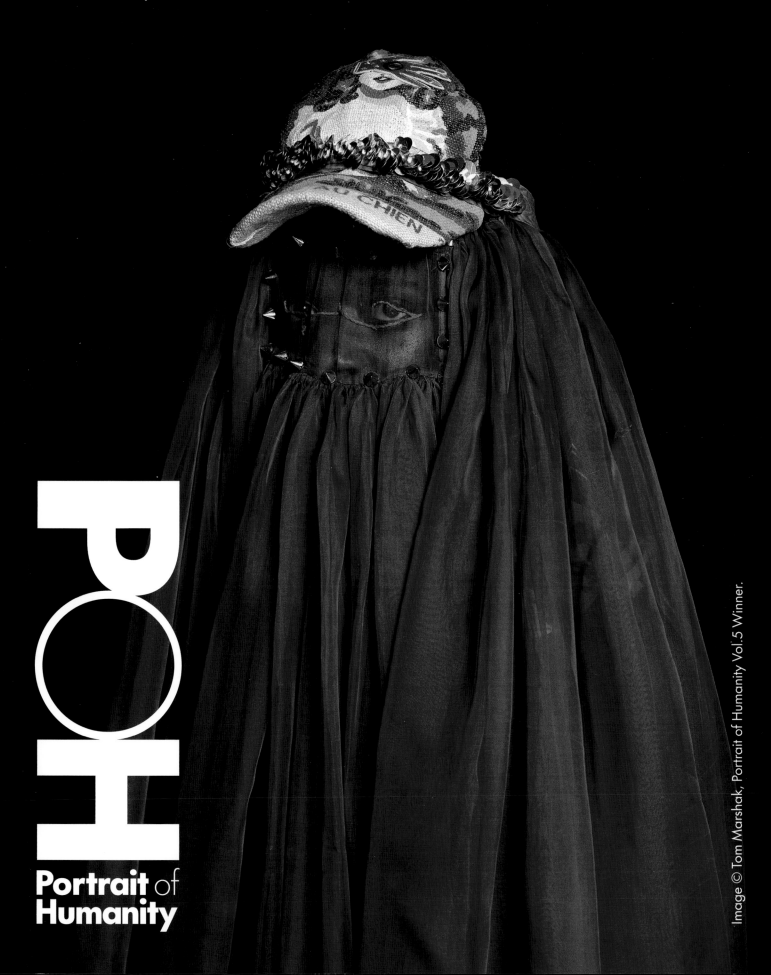

23 Nov 2023 – 07 Jan 2024
State Art Gallery, Hyderabad
www.indianphotofest.com/exhibitions

INDIAN
PHOTO
FESTIVAL

POH
Portrait of
Humanity

Image © Tom Marshak, Portrait of Humanity Vol.5 Winner.

THE
PORT
ISS

PHOTOGRAPHIC COLLABORATION COMES IN MANY FORMS, FROM FAST-PACED MAGAZINE SHOOTS TO CREATIVE COMPANIONSHIP IN KOLKATA WITH **SOHAM GUPTA**. **MICKALENE THOMAS** AND **NADAV KANDER** LEAD US DEEP INTO THEIR PORTRAITURE, **CAMILLE GHARBI** TALKS PHOTO TESTIMONY BEHIND BARS, **SUSAN MEISELAS** AND **WENDY EWALD** CONSIDER POWER DYNAMICS, AND WE LOOK AT COMMUNITY-BUILDING AMONG THE **QUEER NEW WAVE**

RAIT
UE

REFRAME
THE
PORTRAIT

RE-ENVISAGING PHOTOGRAPHIC
PORTRAITURE THROUGH HER
IMAGES, COLLAGES, AND
CURATORIAL AND MENTORING
ACTIVITIES, **MICKALENE THOMAS**
MAKES THE CASE FOR A WIDER
REIMAGINING OF SOCIETY
WORDS BY **ELISA MEDDE**

Opposite: *Jet Blue #31*, 2021.

Right: *Courbet #3 (Sleep)*, 2011.

Page 72 top: *Portrait of Din #4*, 2015.

Page 72 below: *November 1971*, 2019.

Page 73: *Portrait of Solange Sitting on Edge of Couch*, 2013.

Page 74: *Shug Kisses Celie*, 2016.

Page 75: *Nus Exotiques #2*, 2023.

As soon as the Zoom call starts, Mickalene Thomas' smile fills the screen. She greets me with a warm "Hello", immediately followed by "Sorry, but this is going to be a bit on the move". She is on the phone in her house, preparing to get in a car to reach her next appointment, due in a little more than an hour. I see she is busy, yet I feel I have her total attention. While her body moves around – gets the jacket, looks for keys – her voice is calm. Focused. Welcoming. In my mind I picture her as Durga, a major Hindu goddess associated with strength, protection and motherhood, but also destruction, so as to empower creation.

I am reminded of something Pulitzer Prize winner Salamishah Tillet wrote in a text accompanying Thomas' work in *Foam Magazine* a couple of years ago. The text opens with Tillet describing a visit to Thomas' studio, where she asked Thomas about a recently made collage opening the documentary *Toni Morrison: The Pieces I Am*. In response, Thomas opened her file box and started pulling out bits and pieces of images, fragments of old photos, large quantities of remnants kept in case they might come in handy, but all pieces that had contributed to the making of her collages. In that moment Tillet understood how Thomas' practice, that restless, continuous collection, disruption and rescuing of traces and fragments, betrayed "the secret of her genius". "So you actually think in collage, don't you?" she asked.

I mention this anecdote and ask Thomas the same question. "Oh wow, that would be a big question," she laughs. "Often, my thoughts are very abstract and I try to articulate and bring everything together in a cohesive way. And I think it's because I'm always thinking of different things, concepts, ideas, consecutively. It's beneficial to my working process and the way I make things. So I'm able to work on multiple things at once and see them through to completion, to the level where they both have the same amount of thoughtfulness and consideration, inventiveness and experimentation. This excites me because it allows me to move around my ideas and work, but it also allows me to pull from one aspect of what I'm working on to another and bring it over."

My first encounter with Thomas was in 2019, in the circumstances relating to Tillet's text. Back then I was editor-in-chief of *Foam Magazine*, and working with Mariama Attah on what would be the Play! issue, a publication themed around playing, its subversive potential, and its relation to how we experience the world and its power structures. That year had been an incredible one for Thomas – she had just been honoured with the Pioneer Works Visionary Award, and at the Muse Aperture Gala for "her brilliant use of the photographic image to assert new definitions of beauty and Black female identity, celebrity and sexuality".

Her works were also already in the collections of MoMA, the National Portrait Gallery, Smithsonian American

"I PULL FROM ARCHIVAL IMAGES TO SEEK SUBJECTS FROM THE PAST, THEN WITH NEW IMAGES CHANGE THE VIEWER'S PERCEPTION OF WHAT THEY KNEW. THESE COMPLICATED, COMPLEX AND CHALLENGING HISTORIES NEED TO BE BROUGHT FORWARD"
MICKALENE THOMAS

Art Museum, Solomon R Guggenheim Museum, Whitney Museum of American Art, and the Studio Museum in Harlem. Attah and I had both been following and admiring her work for a while, since Aperture published her first book, *Muse: Mickalene Thomas Photographs*, in 2015, followed in 2016 by a solo show at the Aperture Gallery titled *Muse: Mickalene Thomas Photographs and tête-à-tête*. That was the moment she established a different relationship with photography in her practice, and not only because *Muse* was one of her first exhibitions to contain exclusively photographic work, beyond her well-established oeuvre in painting. In fact, the large-scale photographs, collages and Polaroids included in the show were all produced between 2001 and 2015, testimony to her constant involvement and experimentation with the medium since early on.

The *tête-à-tête* section of *Muse*, a mini group show within the show, was the second instalment of the namesake exhibition Thomas curated in 2012 at Yancey Richardson Gallery. Inspired by the *Conversation: Among Friends* symposium held at MoMA, Thomas felt pressed to question ideas about collaborative work. As the press release for the show explained: "Mickalene Thomas was interested in the

performative way in which male artists use their physical presence and body in relation to the viewer, and the way many female artists see themselves through the gaze of another (often male)". The artists she selected included LaToya Ruby Frazier, Hank Willis Thomas, Deana Lawson, Zanele Muholi, Clifford Owens, Mahlot Sansosa and Malick Sidibé, among others, next to a selection of Thomas' Polaroids.

The Aperture *tête-à-tête* was oriented towards her approach to collaboration, her celebration of artists she thought had helped nurture her own practice, whose work she felt was in deep dialogue with her own. Remarkably, this edition included works from Carrie Mae Weems, an artist she has always mentioned as deeply important in bringing photography to the core of her art. The Aperture show and accompanying publication were an adjustment in framing, in composition. That was the moment in which all the crucial elements and themes of her poetics aligned, took stage, and started to echo her practice at large – the celebration of the Black female body, its power, beauty and sensuality; the importance of the community, and the necessity to give back, share, empower and create space; the continuous relation with the past and how it informs our present, the gratitude towards the giants' shoulders we stand on, and the urgency to rewrite and heal the violent narratives plaguing generations.

Mixing up media

Thomas was initially known for her paintings, works that ventured into imagination and experiments with mixed media, allowing her to build the physicality and structures to bring that imagination into the world and outside the frame. Photography brought in a sense of the real. I ask what each craft does to the other, and how she balances them out to get exactly where she wants her images to go. "They're different tools in which each medium provides a different access into visibility, and in how we experience the work," she says. "I really think about how the power of those tools could make a difference and will convey the idea in the best way possible – by executing it through that medium.

"Oftentimes, there's a middle space between photography and painting, and each has its own powerful properties. And for me, painting allows for a space of visual fantasy where you can do whatever you want. You can provide narrative to both. Photography lends itself to something that is more believable. We take it as it is. There's an element of truth. We are more familiar to the subject. But all of it is still performative. The familiar artifice of the image allows us to believe all the elements of the photo image and its truthfulness. There's this play between reality and fantasy, an intersection that I integrate into my work. This is the space I enjoy working from. You have these elements that allow you to manipulate the visual perception of the work. That's what creating art is – an illusion. But we often have the illusion more in photography."

The idea of an intersection between reality and illusion is powerful when applied to the remediation of archival and vernacular imagery, used not only as a stylistic reference but also, and especially, in a critical way. There is the radical mental and aesthetic act of representing and celebrating the Black body, in a way that recalls and reappropriates the majesty of French classical portraiture. Then there is the rehabilitation of archival imagery, and the confrontation with the narratives and tropes they possess and convey, from 19th-century plates to 1950s French magazines.

We talk about the process that led to her most recent series *je t'adore*, presented at Yancey Richardson, which includes 13 large-scale mixed-media photo collages, inspired by the imagery of Black female erotica featured in 1950s French publication *Nus Exotiques* and *Jet* magazine calendars. I ask about her relation with researching archival materials, and their historical reception and narratives.

"I pull from archival images to seek subjects from the past, then with new images change the viewer's perception of what they knew. These complicated, complex and challenging histories need to be brought forward," she explains. "In a way, it's like being an archaeologist. You're discovering information, excavating and bringing that up to the surface so that the new generation can understand particular histories, moments and visual aesthetics. It's really the need to see myself in others.

"Discovering that really excites me. I have to feel something from it. And when I feel something from it, it resonates with me in a way beyond the physical. It becomes very visceral, in a way where I feel like there's a story that could be told. There's a narrative here, there's things that have been unspoken and there's a new platform of agency that can be provided for these images. A new context taking French erotica from the 1950s and paying it forward to the present public, showing ways in which we see ourselves, or how we can see ourselves cross-Atlantic, or how the Black body has been seen within the diaspora.

"Oftentimes, and particularly in America, we want to compartmentalise the notion of what the Black body is, ignoring the diaspora of how Black bodies have moved through the world and what those relationships were and are now. I love juxtaposing the Black body from spaces that are not as familiar to me to familiar ones, like *Jet* calendars, and create a complex conversation for people to look at the differences of how we were being seen, or how we were being looked at. And it's not necessarily about subjugating or exploiting, but really celebrating. Celebrating our bodies, because the bodies and images in those particular times, they look and appear so different than today.

"I think it's really important, especially for young girls, to see that there are bodies of various shapes and sizes that are just beautifully natural and they may look different. Loving all aspects of it; life, sickness, scarification from motherhood, and ageing. I think the notion of body positivity comes through some of these archival images. And it excites me, the act of pulling, excavating those images and presenting them in a way that could be a new, unexplored perspective for young girls to see themselves other than what they're getting from Instagram or social media platforms or magazines. There's a power in these images and I'm so grateful for them."

Expressions of gratitude

The urgency with which Thomas talks about representation runs very deep. I keep thinking, when does representation become celebration? I admire how, not only pose, but also materials come into play in her works as adorning elements – when I look at her works, in whatever medium they were made, words such as celebration, beauty, pleasure come to mind. There is also the idea of 'gratitude' as an ultimate form of love – I see you, thank you for existing.

Thomas' images are acts of love, as are her curatorial and mentoring activities. She recently opened the exhibition *Portrait of an Unlikely Space* at Yale University Art Gallery, which again revolves around the idea of the *Muse* – this

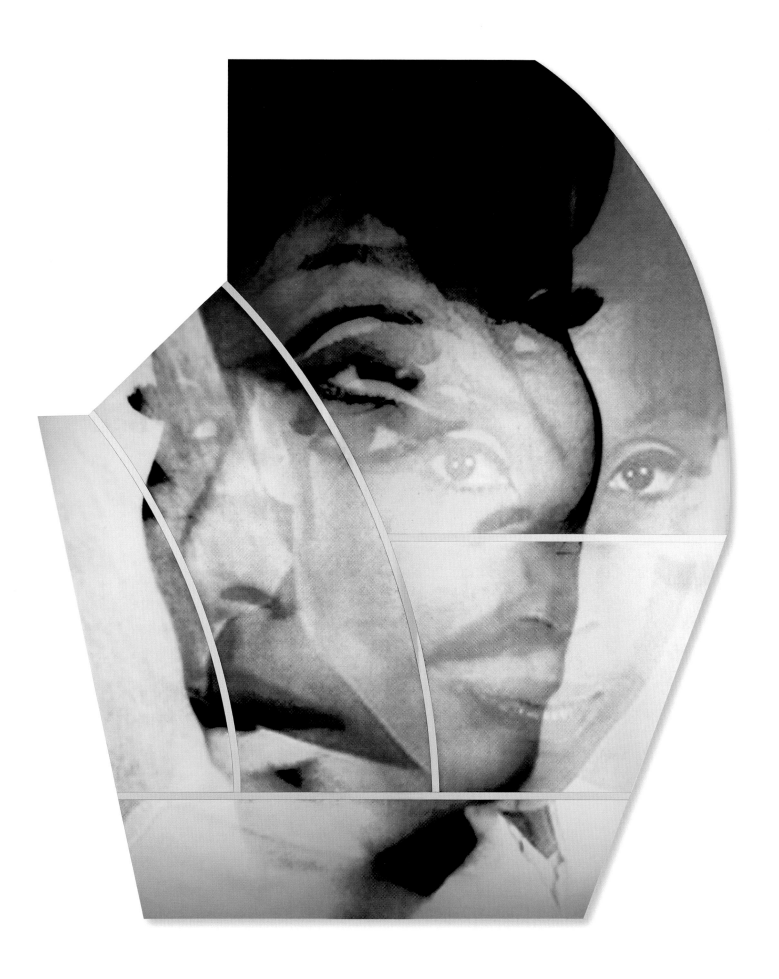

time represented by a single object, a portrait miniature of Rose Prentice, a domestic worker, painted in around 1837. The exhibition addresses imagery of Black people from the pre-emancipation era, and puts rare miniatures, daguerreotypes, silhouettes and engravings in dialogue with the works of eight contemporary artists plus Thomas.

The other artists are the youngest branches of a family tree, as Thomas described it in an interview to *The New York Times*, and include the likes of Lebohang Kganye, Adia Millett and Mary Enoch Elizabeth Baxter. The show, especially Thomas' 2011 Polaroid series, referred to as *Courbet* images, and Baxter's *Consecration To Mary*, give us the chance to talk about the more problematic aspect of archival and historical imagery – the artist's responsibilities. In *Consecration to Mary*, Baxter worked on two 1882 photographs by Thomas Eakins, for example, which exploit a young Black girl posing naked. Baxter inserted herself in the images as if protecting the child, shielding the view to her exposed body.

Thomas explains: "Working from images like Eakins' photographs directly points at the idea of subjectification, the notion of her reclaiming herself. It's almost like saving her,

going back in time and sort of uplifting and carrying her out of that picture. And to me, that's what makes it so powerful. It's like the superhero come in and say, I see you. And now I'm going to claim this space and protect you. I think we have a responsibility when we put images out in the world. As an artist, it is very important for me to create impact and explore a transformative way of how we can see ourselves. And even claiming or reclaiming images through archival printed matter, that's a way for me to make sense of this, to put forth, to feel empowered socially and politically. There's a vulnerability to creating art, but I also feel there's a sense of responsibility."

Thomas moves through words, references and topics just as she creates her artworks, and again, a powerful and benevolent Durga springs to my mind. She is a multitude. As she talks, I see New York City unfolding through the window of the car now carrying her along – a familiar sight, another layer of energy adding to hers. Her thoughts feel like hands with various tools, each of them razor sharp and working towards the same end result. Perhaps this could be summarised as 'doing the work'. Creating artworks, curating exhibitions, mentoring young and underrepresented artists (she co-founded

the Pratt>Forward programme in 2021 to support and provide mentorship and peer-advice emerging artists), buying a train ticket for a stranger at the station; these are all parts of the same practice, one that cares and takes care, that feels the embodiment of bell hooks' visual politics, infused with love.

"People always ask, how are you able to do all these things?" she tells me. "You do it because you can, because you care, and you just make it so much easier for someone else. I'm where I'm at because someone, somewhere, made it easy for me to develop, to create art – they opened the door. At some point, whether inconsequential or consequential, whether I can see it or not, someone made a difference. Someone made a decision that I was deserving of this space and time to not have to work at a retail store, so I could work in my studio and make art. That is crucially important."

Reinventing portraiture
Over the years, Thomas has built a practice that has deeply challenged and reinvented the way we think about portraiture, especially in photography. Quoting Carrie Mae Weems, she is doing "What it takes to turn a whole visual narrative, an

art history, upside down rather than simply inserting the Black body in it". In her large-scale tableaux she has created, or rather recreated a space for existence, an ever-changing setting in which her sitters, muses or subjects are celebrated and adorned, reinvented and recognised, empowered and rediscovered. As she eloquently explains her practice, I am reminded of Mark Sealy's thinking of jazz as "disruptive, unanchored space" in which unlearning and reprocessing can happen, at the same time healing and revolutionising.

"I think that does relate to me", she replies. "And I think not only jazz, but hip-hop and avant-garde. That's where I feel like collage comes out of. It comes out of the juxtaposition, the intersection, the zigzag, and creation within disruption, making sense of many things that are happening simultaneously. Just like our world. Whether or not we respond or acknowledge the disparity of others that we see when we walk through the world, we see them. And so we become aware of it. James Baldwin said it very poignantly, that we are everyone, whether we acknowledge that or not. The people that we see in the world, we too are them. We are a reflection of each other." **BJP**

mickalenethomas.com

Portrait of Britain

Comprising 200 remarkable photographs, Portrait of Britain Volume 6 is a testament to the resilience, strength and unity that define the people of the United Kingdom.

Volume 6 is available now at bluecoatpress.co.uk

IN PLAIN SIGHT

CAMILLE GHARBI
PORTRAYS THE PERPETRATORS AND TOOLS OF DOMESTIC VIOLENCE AND THE BEDROOMS OF THOSE WHO ESCAPED – IMAGES OF ORDINARINESS AT ODDS WITH THE BRUTAL ACTIONS OF THE AGGRESSORS

WORDS BY **SARAH MOROZ**

In her book *Everybody*, Olivia Laing writes: "How do you convey the systematisation of violence against women if there is a conspiracy of silence around it, if it is so tolerated and sustained as to have merged with the fabric of ordinary reality?" It is an excruciating question which remains all too relevant around the world, and which French photographer Camille Gharbi wrestles with in her work. Her book, *Facing Up. Stories of Domestic Violence (Faire Face. Histoires de Violences Conjugales)* published by *The Eyes*, gathers three series on domestic violence and its tragically mundane everydayness. In *There's No Such Thing as Monsters (Les monstres n'existent pas)*, made between 2019 and 2022, she tries to unmask this "conspiracy of silence", photographing people who have been convicted or accused of killing their domestic partners. The series includes eight men and one woman either serving sentences or awaiting trial in detention centres when Gharbi photographed them; the ratio loosely reflects the statistics in France where women are disproportionately killed by men.

Gharbi originally studied architecture, working in the field until she was 30. A self-taught photographer, she has "always been attracted to social subjects", particularly what it means to live in a patriarchal society. It is an area in which "it's important to build a relationship of trust, even with ephemeral encounters", she adds, and she often asks her subjects to participate in making the images, discussing how they will look so that they are comfortable with and actively involved in their representation.

There's No Such Thing as Monsters took Gharbi three years to formulate, most of which was dedicated to research with experts such as psychologists, psychiatrists, educators and prison workers. "I had to understand the mechanisms at work," Gharbi explains. "And very quickly, it became obvious to me that the side of the 'bad guys' is fundamental. It's two sides of the same coin – as long as there are abusers, there will be victims."

She made the photographs in a French prison, where she also conducted interviews in the visitation rooms, asking

Continues on page 90

Opposite: *Victoria, 22 years old*, from the series *A Room of One's Own (Une chambre à soi)*, a collection of 50 images and statements taken in the women's refuge FIT Une femme, un Toit (One Woman, One Roof).

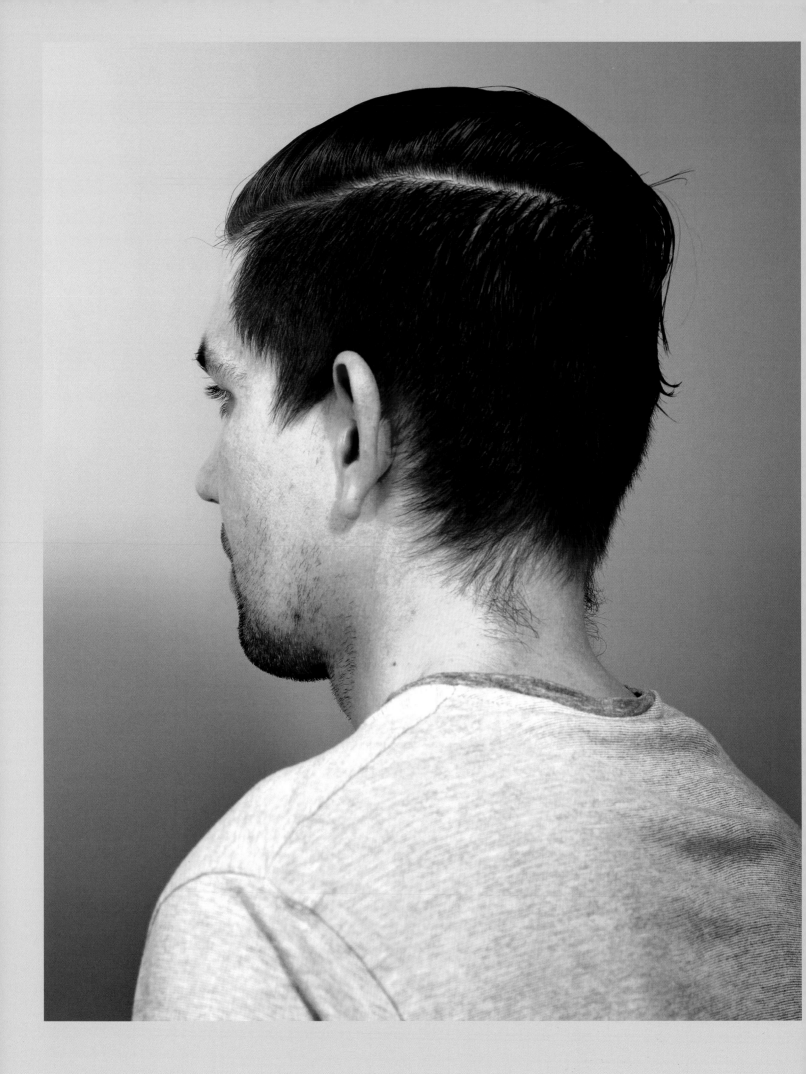

DAMIEN, 31 YEARS OLD
DIGITAL MACHINE OPERATOR AND PROGRAMMER. ELECTRONIC MUSIC PRODUCER AND DJ. SENTENCED TO 25 YEARS FOR MURDERING HIS SPOUSE. IN DETENTION SINCE THE AGE OF 28

"I was never really a violent person, never one to fight. In my family, violence was unknown. No one was violent. No one's ever been to jail before me. Violence only surfaced twice in my relationship. The first time was a few months before the tragedy, and then the second time. That day, I killed her. Ever since I got locked up, I've been trying to figure out how I got to this point.

"I think at one point in our relationship, I sank into depression. I stopped enjoying my job, felt useless. I was working Monday to Saturday, going out on weekends, sleeping maybe five hours a night. I was burned out, lost the meaning in what I was doing... I know that's where it started. I had dreams of travelling, of seeing the world. I had all these ambitions, but actually I built walls around myself. I had a permanent job, and that meant stability. Around me, I saw people struggling to find work. The thought of leaving mine scared me. I was afraid of losing it all and ending up screwed. Leaving felt like risking having to move back in with my parents, which to me would've been admitting failure. This phrase kept echoing in my head: 'You failed.'

"Looking back, it seems completely stupid. But I convinced myself I couldn't do it. I started dreading going to work, but paradoxically, whenever they asked me to put in extra hours on the weekends, I always said yes. I started drinking after work. I closed myself off, put on a front, never admitting I was in a bad place. I never talked about it.

"The absence of communication seeped into my relationship and my life as a whole. I grew up in a family where we keep things to ourselves. I always had to deal with my issues alone. No one ever told me as a kid, 'If something's wrong, you talk to us about it.' And communication can solve so many problems. To feel supported by your family in good times and bad, to have someone to turn to when you're struggling – I had the opposite experience. Since my teens, I've learned to face life's ups and downs on my own. At 12, I started smoking cannabis, and by 14, I was on to heroin. I abused drugs until my 20s, like it was a way out.

"Some months before I crossed the line, after a night out at our friend's place, there was a first episode of violence with my partner. I was heavily intoxicated when it happened. Instead of re-evaluating myself, talking to someone, seeking help, I told myself it wouldn't happen again – and that was that. But I kept drinking after work, I started taking drugs again. I closed off even more. My partner did everything to help me. I couldn't communicate. I let our relationship turn toxic, until we broke up.

"The moment of our break-up was like my world was collapsing. She had become my pillar. I know full well it was my fault that she left, but I failed to realise that when it mattered. And then too, instead of questioning myself, I kept drinking more and more and heavily started using drugs again, until that day. It was three weeks after our break-up. That morning at work, I learned from a friend that she had been with someone else for several months. I was supposed to go to hers that very day to return some of her things. When I got off work at noon, I drank nearly an entire bottle of whiskey before going to see her. We started arguing, and at one point, I completely lost control. It was only afterwards that I grasped the gravity of what had really happened.

"What happened, I think about it all the time. It haunts me relentlessly. It's on me that things reached this point, and the tragic part is someone is gone because of it all. Someone who never asked for any of this and instead did everything to help me. Taking it out on her instead of facing my own demons was an act of utter weakness, and it's something I still don't understand. Why did I take it out on her instead of just ending it all for myself?

"As soon as I got locked up, I knew I had to talk to a psychiatrist right away. I had to figure out how I'd let things get this far. I started to reflect. It became my first mission behind bars, out of respect for my late partner. Often, people are ashamed to talk about their problems. We live in a world that's all about appearances, where you've got to act like everything's great all the time, like you're doing just fine. But here's the thing, the minute people start feeling off, they need to open up right at those first warning signs. There is no shame in it, everyone has problems in life." **BJP**

ROMAIN, 40 YEARS OLD

TRUCK DRIVER. SENTENCED TO 22 YEARS IN PRISON FOR MURDERING A PERSON WHO IS OR HAS BEEN A SPOUSE. IN DETENTION SINCE THE AGE OF 30

"My name is Romain, I'm 40 years old. Outside, I was a truck driver. It's been 10 years since I've been in jail. I'm in prison for murdering a woman. I wanted to speak because I've done a lot of soul-searching since the incident. I feel like maybe my story could be a wake-up call for other guys that violence gets you nowhere. Before prison, I was violent. I never hurt anyone directly, but it was there... I broke things, punched walls. I was impulsive, unable to rein myself in. Quick to frustration, always unsatisfied. Always wanting more. These are traits I've carried since childhood.

"I was a troublesome kid, a disruptor. My parents split when I was born, and I was constantly shuffled between them because of my behaviour. I had a quick temper, couldn't control my agitation, it had to get out, one way or another. And often, it was through violence. Let's face it. I was selfish. That became clear to me in prison. I thought only about myself, my hobbies, my passions. I resisted dialogue, never questioned my actions.

"Before the crime, I spent years in a serious relationship with the mother of my daughter. We were buying a house, our daughter was just 18 months old. Then I met another woman, and the connection was instant. I left everything to be with her. While at the same time me and my ex had been building something strong... But I left without thinking.

"With the new woman, it got complicated quickly. Mostly because of me. There were frequent conflicts, and I was violent, not towards her or anything, but I hit things, lost my temper. I didn't realise then how violent and frightening my behaviour was. It was shocking behaviour. At the time I didn't realise it. Looking back, I've understood that I felt guilty for walking out like that, leaving my daughter and her mother without much thought. After just three months, when she wanted to break up and told me to leave immediately, my world collapsed.

"There's not one night goes by in 10 years of being in prison when I don't think about it. Because I have to live with that now. I think about her family, her friends, especially her daughter. She had a young girl. There's not a day when it doesn't haunt me. And it should, what I did is irreversible. I understand the gravity of my actions and their consequences. I deserve this sentence. I know what I've done. One day, I'll be free, but everything will always trace back to this. It'll have to be talked about again and again. And that's only fair. Otherwise, it would be too easy.

"This sentence has allowed me to learn about myself. It's unfortunate that it took this tragedy for me to question my behaviour. Thanks to therapy and sports, I've learned to control myself. When things aren't going well, I exercise to blow-off steam, read, and take a step back – things I never did before. I don't engage in conflicts with other inmates anymore.

"I refuse to perpetrate any more violence because I know where my violence has led me and the harm it can do. Whenever anger surges, memories of the pain I've inflicted come rushing back. Violence never leads to anything good. Now, I try to spread this awareness in prison. When conflicts arise, I try to defuse them. I try to talk sense into the younger guys. That's my mindset now. Trying to prevent, to help. I want to work with re-entry programmes for youths. Speak at organisations for violent individuals.

"I aim to prevent, to help, to do whatever I can to avoid another tragedy. After doing the worst, I'm trying to do some good. It's the only thing that can give my life meaning now.

"I've lost contact with my daughter. But I accept it, I have no choice. It's probably better for her. I've tattooed her name on my arm so she's with me, despite it all. You only realise what you've lost when it's all gone. It's tragic." BJP

questions conceived with the help of a psychologist. Gharbi says the interviews were key, shedding light on the toxic masculinity at play: the way these men were instructed to be self-sufficient and shun help, their unshakeable posturing for absolute control, and often highlighting their addiction to drugs or alcohol.

Many of those Gharbi interviewed came from backgrounds blighted by domestic violence, reproducing in adulthood what they had experienced as children. Many expressed regret for not having found a psychologist earlier, or not having sought help for addiction, or taken steps towards recovery. The photographs and testimonies function jointly as diptychs, "each part having the same weight," Gharbi emphasises.

"There are very few true psychopaths," she states, although abusive partners are commonly designated as crazy. "That's the image that predominates the collective imagination," she adds. "It's a way to flush away the issue, to say, 'These people are monsters, we can't do much else but lock them up. We can't do anything with crazy people'. But there are plenty of things we can seek out to improve the situation."

Many sides of abuse
Gharbi selected her subjects carefully, seeking out individuals who had admitted their guilt, and were actively questioning themselves and their motives. Most people who commit femicide do not own up to what they have done, she says, a reaction very specific to this kind of crime. People who have robbed banks often freely admit to their actions, but those who have killed their partners tend to invert the culpability, and minimise their own part.

The small pool Gharbi found comprised individuals of varied ages and social profiles, from different geographical locations and professional backgrounds. In fact, she says, "there wasn't one person who didn't surprise me – it's disturbing". Her words echo Carmen Maria Machado's insights from *In the Dream House*, a memoir of a damaging lesbian relationship. "Abusers do not need to be, and rarely are, cackling maniacs," writes Machado. "They just need to want something and not care how they get it."

Gharbi's images are deliberately ambiguous, each figure turned three-quarters away "to suggest, rather than offer a full portrait". There are contours of the faces, silhouettes of the clothes, an unfaltering and also unsettling sense of the everyman. Domestic abusers cannot just be recognised at will; when a certain kind of violence is endemic, the point is that it is widespread.

Gharbi had other reasons to photograph them this way, however: partly to protect their identities, very definitely to avoid putting them on a pedestal, but also to allow each individual to stand in for any domestic abuser. Working within the limited means of the prison, she wanted to "avoid the pitfalls of sensationalist photo, to remain as sober and as distanced as possible".

Left: From the series *Acts of Love (Preuves d'amour)*, 2018, a collection of 20 photographs challenging "understanding and response to domestic violence by shedding light on its most extreme manifestation: intimate partner femicide". When exhibited, Gharbi includes the names and details of individuals who have been killed with the depicted everyday objects.

Opposite: *Debora, 24 years old*, from the series *A Room of One's Own (Une chambre à soi)*, a collection of 50 images and statements taken in the women's refuge FIT Une femme, un Toit (One Woman, One Roof).

love

Left: *Mina's Room*, from the series *A Room of One's Own* (*Une chambre à soi*), taken in the women's refuge FIT Une femme, un Toit (One Woman, One Roof).

All images © Camille Gharbi.

Further action

If you have been affected by anything in this article, there are several organisations that can help, including Women's Aid, Refuge and more.
womensaid.org.uk
refuge.org.uk

"WE ACCLIMATE TO VISUALS OF VIOLENCE. I THINK THE 'SHOCK IMAGE' IS NO LONGER THE BEST WAY TO REACH PEOPLE IN OUR ERA... IT STARTLES YOU IN THE MOMENT, BUT YOU DON'T WANT TO LIVE WITH A DIFFICULT IMAGE"
CAMILLE GHARBI

This sense of neutrality seems almost implausible when faced with such perpetrators. How did Gharbi achieve this state when dealing with femicide, the zenith of misogyny? "You have to be angry, but you can't be blinded by anger," she explains. She spoke to the subjects, she adds, but was also clear "not to have a debate, not to intervene personally – just ask key questions to get them to talk. It was hard not to respond in anger, but it was a necessity in this work."

In her introduction to the series, Gharbi reveals more, explaining that she asked those she photographed why they thought they were in prison, and what they were doing to change. For her, the latter is key. "They're photographed in prison, they're being punished for what they've done, as defined by society," she says. "They will leave prison – what will happen then? The idea is for people to come out better, not worse."

Away from the shock
Gharbi avoided making emotive images, pivoting away from the affecting legacy of Donna Ferrato's 1991 work *Living With the Enemy* or Nan Goldin's multi-decade *The Ballad of Sexual Dependency*. Her work has more in common with Laia Abril's ongoing project *A History of Misogyny*, which uncovers violence against women with clinical clarity. "We acclimate to visuals of violence," Gharbi points out. "I think the 'shock image' is no longer the best way to reach people in our era." For her, the current saturation of attention-grabbing, sensationalist images can bleed into sheer voyeurism, further distancing us from the topics they are meant to illuminate. "The 'shock image' startles you in the moment, but you don't want to live with a difficult image," she says. "Even images of war – we need them, but they don't have the same effect as 50 years ago."

Gharbi does not dismiss difficult images, the depictions that leave a trace, but has a different goal for her work. Aiming to open a space of reflection, to get people's attention and inspire a meaningful empathy, she chooses to use 'quiet' images. The three series comprising *Facing Up* "reinforce the everydayness of suffering", the ugliness of femicides "both so present and so badly represented". These series were made in succession, but were not initially seen as one project: *There's No Such Thing as Monsters*, from 2022, is the most recent. The first was *Acts of Love (Preuves d'amour)* in 2018, in which Gharbi catalogued everyday objects transformed into weapons, an idea that came to her after reading about a case involving a box cutter utility knife. As an architect she was used to seeing box cutters, she says ("It was a tool I was familiar with in the day-to-day"), but now it was being used in a more sinister way.

Approaching a French feminist association for more information, she carried on researching for months, uncovering other banal objects put to violent ends – including a scarf, a plastic bag and a pillow. The series was published in *Le Monde* in 2020 and widely exhibited, and went on to win a prize at French photojournalism festival Visa pour l'image.

In her next series, *A Room of One's Own (Une chambre à soi)*, 2020–21, she pondered how to show victims but transcend victimhood, how to represent without stereotyping, how to uphold and illuminate their strength. She made photographs in a refuge shelter in Paris that welcomes women aged 18 to 25 who have endured domestic and/or sexual and/or familial violence. Given their young age, "they should be building their identity, but they're already rebuilding their identity," Gharbi notes, adding, "I didn't want to entrap them."

She decided to capture the shelter's bedrooms without their occupants, creating portraits in absentia which record the first safe spaces the young women escaped to. The rooms range from chaotic to cutesy, some touchingly adolescent with their oversized stuffed animals and bright Post-it notes. "It shows them without showing them," Gharbi says.

The website of Féminicides France (feminicides.fr) includes a tally for the disturbing number of femicides registered each year in France (80 up to September in 2023), while the collective #NousToustes (noustoutes.org) organises conferences and roundtables around sexism and sexual violence. But while there are good forces at work, the wider system of justice is flawed. As Gharbi notes: "You receive a less severe punishment for hitting your wife than for having drugs on your person."

Domestic violence is not punished at an appropriate scale but, while this is infuriating, the solution cannot come through punishment alone. Preventing repeat offences requires breaking the cycle of violence, a process that will need colossal changes in society and education in France and beyond. Gharbi hopes her work can help in this process, and chooses to show it in prisons and schools as well as festivals and galleries. Ideally, she wants to provoke discussions that might lead to new perceptions. "I don't believe in radical change, but art and photography can contribute to change," she says. "I am persuaded of that." **BJP**

camillegharbi.com

SOHAM GUPTA MADE HIS NAME CAPTURING KOLKATA'S UNSEEN POOR. NOW HIS MOOD HAS SOFTENED, AND THE CITY'S YOUTH MOVEMENT HAS PICKED UP PACE. *DESI BOYS* TELLS THE STORY

WORDS BY **RAVI GHOSH**

STREET STYLE

In Kolkata, young men crowd on roadsides, around food stalls, in shops, warehouses and arcades. From the tomb of Wajid Ali Shah – the last Nawab of the northern region of Awadh – in Metiabruz, to the bustle of Park Street and Mullick Bazar, men linger on motorbikes, smoke, laugh and flirt nervelessly, the same as youngsters the world over. One of them, Sahid, looks especially gleeful, his shirt removed to reveal a toned torso and a forearm tattoo sleeve (the word 'Love' is just visible). A woman places her ringed fingers on his bare chest, their easy smiles matching. Her eyes are relaxed, looking directly into the camera, while Sahid peers over his muscular right shoulder. His body, her face, are almost luminous against the night sky and worn paintwork of the thick railings behind them.

Sahid is an amateur bodybuilder, we learn from Soham Gupta's *Desi Boys* journals. He has just started working in his father's motorcycle garage in Tollygunge in south Kolkata, but often hangs out at the Safari Park in nearby Rabindra Sarobar – one of countless public areas or monuments named after Rabindranath Tagore in the city. "The girls are always dying to pose with me – and it always gives me a high," Sahid says. After he has posed for Gupta, Sahid takes him to meet some of his friends nearby, boasting to them that he has just had his picture taken. "The others wanted to have their images made and I was suddenly engulfed in requests, from all sides," Gupta writes. "And happily, I kept making images."

These are the Desi Boys – Gupta's friends, inspiration, subjects. They come from across this city of nearly 15 million, a swelling youth movement comprising both Muslims and Hindus belonging to a range of caste positions, including some Dalits. The idea for the project came about after Gupta was shooting a fashion editorial for New Delhi-based magazine *Platform*, where he was commissioned by Bharat Sikka. He began noticing what had previously blended into the background. Not just young men wearing fake designer clothing and dyeing their hair, but the way these sartorial choices constituted a new form of expression – the audacity with which they showed off, exchanged ideas, circulated pictures of each other, and saw their choices as distinctly subcultural. "There are different hints of masculinity in different places," Gupta tells me. "They're playing many different roles."

Music is a key part of this new collective identity. Pune-born rapper MC Stan is an important touchpoint for these groups, Gupta says, with his lyrics describing life in – and beyond – India's working and lower-class communities. The song *Basti Ka Hasti* is especially popular, its lyrics a combination of tribal hip-hop bravado and pride in a disadvantaged upbringing: "*I'm a celebrity in the township!*" he barks at one point. "MC Stan is very explicitly talking about the economic divide in India; he is the ultimate symbol for the Great Indian Dream," Gupta explains. Another rapper crops up in Gupta's journals, an amateur called MC Cidnapper. "He was not older than 20 – with a lock of golden hair up to his shoulder," Gupta writes. The boy bounds over to him, excited that he might have his photograph taken and reciting a few lines from a new song about a girl who left him for a richer man.

New India

Desi Boys depicts a globalised India, but not in the way one might associate with tech-hubs, Silicon Valley CEOs and the country's recent lunar landing, which prime minister Narendra Modi described as "mirror[ing] the aspirations and

"THERE'S NO ROOM FOR XENOPHOBIA IN WEST BENGAL – WE GREW UP AMONG TOO MANY HAMMERS AND SICKLES"
SOHAM GUPTA

capabilities of 1.4 billion Indians". Instead, the globalisation the Desi Boys experience relates mostly to liberalisation, social connectivity and employment – all of which have come about via mass mobile phone uptake in the past decade. In supremely competitive higher education and job markets, the arrival of the gig economy has offered new routes out of unemployment. The criss-crossing journeys these jobs involve add to *Desi Boys'* sense of motion – of restlessness in a hyperactive city, of youthful excitement matched by its surroundings. "For many bourgeois and upper-class families, these boys are looked upon as a menace," Gupta says. That, more than anything else, surely boosts their subcultural credentials.

Desi Boys was made in a specific Indian – and Kolkatan – context. Despite the fake Gucci clothes and Levi's T-shirts, it is a simplification to assume that globalisation means simply emulating the west. There are other motifs alongside the preference for South Asian hip-hop. Several of Gupta's encounters happen while searching for the next bowl of steaming biryani, while buildings' pastel walls, DIY advertising boards and the boys' sandals and coiffed hairstyles are distinctly Indian. The flash illuminates sections of the graffitied walls behind each of Gupta's subjects. Exposed pipes and security grills speak to the thousands of vendors who line Kolkata's daily markets. The youngsters smoke and flex their muscles, gestures whose universality as expressions of young masculinity give them an endearing edge. It is clear that there is a deep affection between artist and subject. "We are like brothers," Gupta reflects.

The role of religion
But more than any visual cues, it is India's tense political and religious climate that gives *Desi Boys* its texture. Led by Modi since 2014, the country's ruling Bharatiya Janata Party (BJP) has proposed a series of legislation which disadvantages India's Muslim population. Passed in 2019, the Citizenship (Amendment) Act (CAA) excluded Muslims from a fast-track for persecuted minorities to attain citizenship, while an accompanying amendment to the National Register of Citizens (NRC) similarly planned to exclude Muslims from an accelerated naturalisation process. Following widespread protests in early 2020, the NRC has yet to be implemented nationwide, with West Bengal among several states not under BJP control saying it will not enact the rulings. Cities with historically Muslim names have been renamed to reflect the BJP's Hindutva ideology – Allahabad has become Prayagraj; Osmanabad is now officially Dharashiv, for example – and mob intimidation and violence against Muslims has become increasingly normalised.

The Desi Boys belong to both religions, and Kolkata's political history plays an important part in the social harmony of the project. West Bengal was led by the communist Left Front from 1977 until 2011. "There's no room for xenophobia in West Bengal – we grew up among too many hammers and sickles," Gupta says. He recalls a discussion with a young man after he commented on his celebratory dress: "Eid is for the Muslims, but at the same time Eid is for everyone." Gupta connects this environment to the willingness of the Desi Boys to express themselves, especially with styles that subvert a traditionally conservative culture. "Here, people feel safe to assert themselves, to go out in clothes that they like, to dye their hair. *Desi Boys* is a response against the xenophobic phase we're going through," he says.

Gupta describes *Desi Boys'* subjects as "all subaltern in some way". He draws a link with his 2017 project *Angst*, in which he made pictures of those at the foot of Kolkata's social and caste ladders – the homeless and the hopeless. The word 'subaltern' resonates deeply in Kolkata, particularly in its adoption by late-20th-century postcolonial theory. Ranajit Guha, Partha Chatterjee and Gayatri Spivak, founding members of the Subaltern Studies group, all attended Kolkata's Presidency College (the latter two were also born in the city) before developing their ideas abroad. The group applied Antonio Gramsci's idea of the subaltern to the marginalised populations whose experiences had been omitted from the history of India, especially narratives of how anti-imperial thought had developed into the independence movement. The subaltern is not simply someone who is poor, neglected or part of a system-based underclass. It means that they are excluded from the economic, social and cultural institutions of power within their colonial society, and – as Spivak queries – may also lack the means to articulate their condition if the language and norms of the coloniser have been impressed upon them.

Subaltern experiences
How does the subaltern relate to Gupta's subjects – and his wider project? On the one hand, his photographs are the voice of subaltern experience. The way Gupta makes pictures is collaborative, but not prescriptive. The boys ask for their portraits for their WhatsApp pictures: "Come, take a group photo – of all of us! And you better send them to us! Not just one or two, but the entire set!" they tell him. His portraits perhaps circulate among his subjects more than they do in a western context, in which exploitative power dynamics risk being repeated. The image is networked, not static.

But still there is wariness around the ethics of display, particularly with *Angst* – the portraits at times shocking, raw and near-theatrical in their depiction of alterity and deprivation. The series was included in the 2019 Venice Biennale, the epitome of western art-world polish. But, as shown by the displacement of street vendors before the recent G20 Summit in New Delhi, the Indian establishment often chooses to look away from its own working classes. In this context, looking at people is recognising that they exist, even if it risks showing them as object not subject. To share images today is to engage with a specific moment in Indian history, to show integration, joy and modernity when openness seems on the wane. It is history without the responsibility of history; a record without the dryness of documentary.

When Gupta first titled *Desi Boys*, he was cautioned by Colin Pantall, a critic who acts as a mentor. Gupta paraphrases his advice in the *Desi Boys* journals. "How can you name it *Desi Boys*! You're further marginalising the subaltern by calling this work that!" But Gupta's photographs can be seen as a subaltern source – as history from below, with photography a new discourse. "*Angst* was made at a time when I was really emotionally down. It had all my anger in the work for a world that doesn't care for people who are marginalised," Gupta says. *Desi Boys* reflects a mood shift, but a way to invite his subjects into the image-making contract. "I'm more balanced now and it shows in the pictures," Gupta continues. "They're a celebration of life – my version of the truth that I am trying to portray." **BJP**

soham-gupta.com

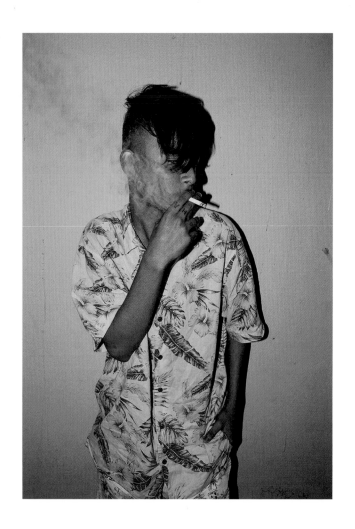

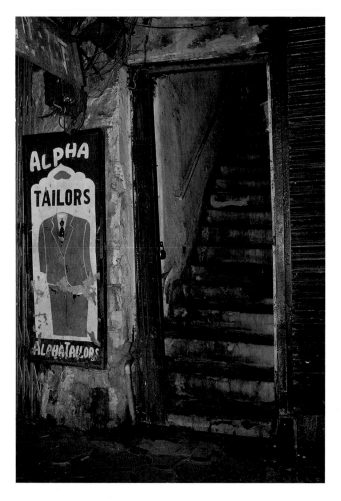

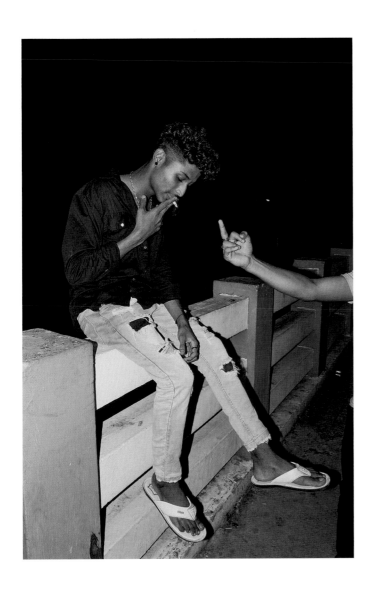

Opposite: From the series *Angst*.

All other images from the series *Desi Boys*.

All images © Soham Gupta.

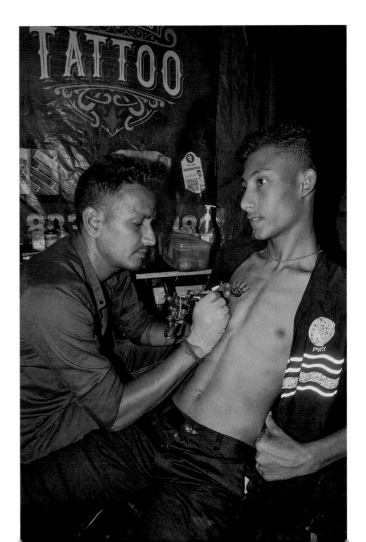

WORDS BY **DIANE SMYTH**

GATHERING HUNDREDS OF PHOTOGRAPHERS, WRITERS AND CRITICS, A NEW BOOK CHALLENGES THE EXISTING NARRATIVES ON PHOTOGRAPHIC HISTORY AND COLLABORATION. WE SPEAK TO TWO OF ITS AUTHORS, **SUSAN MEISELAS** AND **WENDY EWALD**, ABOUT THE RELATIONSHIPS BETWEEN ARTIST AND SUBJECT

POWER PLAYS

On 13 March 2021, Patsy Stevenson attended a vigil in London for Sarah Everard, a young woman who had been raped and killed by a serving police officer. The event took place during a Covid-19 lockdown in which gatherings were subject to harsh restrictions, so it was not officially sanctioned. Hundreds congregated anyway, and the police violently intervened. Stevenson found herself handcuffed and face-down on the ground, and the next day photographs of her arrest hit the front pages.

In September 2023, Stevenson received an official apology from the Met Police, and was paid "substantial damages". Her vindication followed a lengthy legal battle but, she told *The Guardian*, one of the worst aspects of the whole experience had been the photographs, and the way people seemed to perceive them. "Some people were like, 'Oh, you look so great', or 'Your hair looks amazing in that picture'," she told the newspaper. "But that was a really traumatic event for me and I don't think people always take into consideration that I'm not a picture, I'm a person."

Stevenson's story is thought-provoking in many ways, but for photographers it suggests a responsibility when making images. Photographs of people are exactly that – photographs

Left: *Jane Stallard – I Took a Picture With the Statue in my Backyard*, 1980, from the series *Portraits and Dreams* © Wendy Ewald.

of people – but somehow those 'subjects' can get lost in plain sight. As a new book, *Collaboration: A Potential History of Photography*, points out: "Photography generally requires the labour of more than one person. Most of the time, however, the participation of the others who share the work, including the photographed persons, their labour and the ways they envision their participation and negotiate the photographic situations of being together through, with, against and alongside photography, are often disregarded or unnoticed."

The text is a group effort from the team behind *Collaboration* – Ariella Aïsha Azoulay, Leigh Raiford, Laura Wexler, Susan Meiselas and Wendy Ewald – but it draws on ideas from Azoulay's wider output, which proposes an at times radical rethink of photography. Elsewhere she has written that photographs are "unruly metonymical records of an encounter of those convened around the camera" (*Capitalism and the Camera*, 2021), and that cameras are "an imperial technology of extraction" (*Potential History: Unlearning Imperialism*, 2019).

But the authors behind *Collaboration* include two photographers, both of whom are still active today, and as its subtitle suggests, the project is an attempt to both reshape how we think about images and propose new ways to make and share them. *Collaboration* is less a condemnation of photography than a thorough reappraisal of how it works and how we have interpreted it, and a bid to find more equitable approaches. As its introduction says: "We hope that this book can inspire you to experiment with and find the joy in being with others with and through photography."

Collaboration was dreamed up more than a decade ago by Meiselas and Ewald, who have both worked with photography for over 50 years and have long had concerns about the medium's power dynamics. Meiselas' first major project, *Carnival Strippers*, included extensive interviews with the women she was photographing, for example, while in *Portraits and Dreams*, started in 1976, Ewald handed cameras to children and asked them to shoot their own lives.

"I would say that the root of my ambivalence about photography, right from the beginning, was the power of the camera over and in the act of representation," says Meiselas, who joined Magnum Photos in 1976 and became a full member in 1980. "It was right away problematic for me, and I know it was for Wendy too. We've known each other for a long time and, one time when Wendy was staying at mine, we started to reflect on our practice. We found we had similar reference points, and that was very interesting to us. That was an important premise, so we stayed in touch on it, and really reflected on it over the years."

"Then we started to think, 'Well, who's going to write about this?'" laughs Ewald. "Because we knew it wouldn't be us. We met Ariella at around the same time, and both instinctively said, 'OK, we have to talk to her', because she seemed to match and complement the ways we were thinking. We had been focused on our own timeframe, on becoming makers and the work we had seen around us, but she forced us to think about deeper history. We started to see real potential for the project to grow, so we invited Laura and Leigh to join."

The finished book includes images dating back to the start of photography, from 19th century images of female 'hysterics' taken in Salpêtrière Hospital in France through to Dorothea Lange's iconic images of the 'migrant mother in California' and beyond. As the accompanying texts point out, these images are iconic yet somehow unseen, the people

they depict made visible yet also overlooked. The 'hysterics' are seen in terms of symptoms rather than as women or even individuals, while Florence Owens Thompson in Lange's famed image is described by her social position, and usually deprived of her name.

Collaboration includes a quote from Owens Thompson, in which she eloquently explains why she disliked her portrait. "I'm tired of being a symbol of human misery; moreover, my living conditions have improved," she states. "I didn't get anything out of it. I wish she hadn't taken my picture... She didn't ask my name. She said she wouldn't sell the pictures. She said she'd send me a copy. She never did."

The book also includes a spread on the portraits of 'Papa' Renty Taylor and his daughter Delia, which were at the centre of a milestone lawsuit against Harvard University in 2019. The case was brought by Tamara Lanier, who demanded restitution of the daguerreotypes of her ancestors on the grounds that the images were seized from them while they were enslaved; these images were made through a collaboration between Louis Agassiz, the head of Harvard Scientific School, who attempted to use photography to support his racist beliefs, and the photographer JT Zealy. A quote from Lanier in the book states: "For years, Papa Renty's slave owners profited from his suffering, it's time for Harvard to stop doing the same thing to our family."

The changing dynamic

Each chapter in *Collaboration* is arranged chronologically, but the book also features plenty of contemporary work, more positive examples of which include series by Meiselas and Ewald plus self-portraits by Nona Faustine, collaborative portraits by Endia Beal, shots gathered from Iraqis by Geert van Kesteren after the Iraq War, and Carolyn Drake's participatory work with the Uyghur community in China, in which they drew on her images. Each project is given a spread and, where possible, the accompanying texts include comments from the people in the images and their names, as well as comments from the photographers. There are also texts by writers such as Abigail Solomon-Godeau, David Levi Strauss and Mark Sealy, plus voices from a new generation of thinkers.

"We have not stopped with the photographers' 'intentions' or 'statements', but rather we look at those photographic events as they unfold over time," explains the book's introduction. "Attending to the mode of participation of the photographed persons, in particular, enabled us to reconfigure also the participation of the photographers, not as solo masters but rather as parties to the event of photography. We have refused to diminish or deny the collective effort."

This approach de-centres the photographer, and the eight chapters emphasise this with titles such as *The Photographed Person Was Always There*, or *Reshaping the Authorial Position*. Other 'clusters' draw attention to more negative uses of the camera, with tags such as *Sovereign and*

Opposite: The origins of *Collaboration* lie in a series of workshops, talks, lectures and exhibitions in various locations.

"I WOULD SAY THAT THE ROOT OF MY AMBIVALENCE ABOUT PHOTOGRAPHY, RIGHT FROM THE BEGINNING, WAS THE POWER OF THE CAMERA OVER AND IN THE ACT OF REPRESENTATION. IT WAS RIGHT AWAY PROBLEMATIC FOR ME, AND I KNOW IT WAS FOR WENDY [EWALD] TOO" **SUSAN MEISELAS**

Below: From the series *Carnival Strippers*
© Susan Meiselas.

Right: Spreads from the *Collaboration* book –
from top: *Closed Circuit?* AH Wheeler/Cindy
Sherman/Mark Seliger/Paul Mpagi Sepuya/
Shutter Release; *Theorizing Photography in
Front of the Camera* James P Ball/Samuel
J Miller & Others/Frederick Douglass; *Playing
with the Camera* Alfred Stieglitz/Irving Penn/
Ansel Adams/Todd Webb/Georgia O'Keeffe.

CLOSED CIRCUIT?

A.H. Wheeler / Cindy Sherman / Mark Seliger / Paul Mpagi Sepuya / Shutter Release

Everyone thinks these are self-portraits but they aren't meant to be. Cindy Sherman

I'm always present in the work. Paul Mpagi Sepuya

A. H. Wheeler, 'Wheeler's Freak,' Berlin, Wisconsin, 1890

A composite photograph showing a photographic studio interior. One man is seated on a stool near an adjustable clamp to hold his head steady during a long portrait exposure. The second man, standing near to a large view camera, looks like the person being photographed.

The same man is photographed twice by alternately blocking one side of the camera's lens.

I just use myself as a model because I know I can push myself to extremes, make each shot as ugly or goofy or silly as possible. I never thought I was acting. When I became involved with close-ups I needed more information in the expression. I couldn't depend on background or atmosphere. I wanted the story to come from the face. Somehow the acting just happened... I feel I'm anonymous in my work. When I look at the pictures, I never see myself... Sometimes I disappear. Cindy Sherman

Cindy Sherman, Untitled #365, 1976/2000 from the series 'Bus Riders'

Paul Mpagi Sepuya, FIGURE (0X5A0818) 2019

I think of becoming a different person. I look into a mirror next to the camera...it's trance-like. By staring into it I try to become that character through the lens... When I see what I want, my intuition takes over—both in the 'acting' and in the editing. Seeing that other person that's up there, that's what I want, it's like magic. Cindy Sherman

My studio was private, but not a closed environment. Rather, it was a stage that I inhabited and opened to those around me. Paul Mpagi Sepuya

Mark Seliger, Cindy Sherman from the series 'In My Stairwell' February 7, 2005

Paul Mpagi Sepuya, DROP SCENE (_1050630), 2016

I think of becoming a different person... ...

None of the work has been about defining or sort of visualizing through image an identity that could be applied or a label that could be applied. But it is about, in my attempt, I would say, to situate queerness and Blackness as starting points for having to look at photography from the ground up. Paul Mpagi Sepuya

THE ENTANGLED HISTORIES of ethnography and pornography would appear to tell us all we need to know about how the camera looks at women and people of color. To be sure, these conventions by which the racialized and sexualized other has been exposed, scrutinized, and enjoyed by a controlling gaze were established within colonial modernity well before the invention of photography. But the apparatus of photography has left an archive of images whose complicity with power and desire is unsurpassed in its breadth and durability. Indeed, so comprehensive is the authority of this archive, that today we lack any access to a purportedly 'natural' way of looking that has been formed outside or before the machinations of power. The camera, it can be said without exaggeration, is a paradigmatic of visual modernity. Understanding this, what can nevertheless be done to subvert its objectification of the racialized and gendered body?

These two contemporary American photographers, Cindy Sherman and Paul Mpagi Sepuya, have distinguished themselves, in this respect, with various approaches to exposing and experimenting with the photographic stance. For her part, Sherman has decisively shaped the history of art photography since the 1970s by demanding we look again at the dynamic between photographer and sitter. Whereas the genre of the self-portrait has tended to approach this dynamic as containing within it the revelation of the artist's personality and inner depth, Sherman's early images instead mimicked movie stills: she inserted herself into a series of conventionalized stances in which her subjectivity could, by contrast, disappear. Rejecting the idea that her photographs are self-portraits at all, Sherman instead sees them as opportunities to demonstrate the plasticity of the body under the contortions of frame, pose, make-up, and illusion.

Sepuya likewise makes images that are saturated with both desire and referentiality, photos that foil any attempt to resolve them into statements of identity. In pushing the camera, lens, mirror, backdrop, light, and tripod through a kaleidoscope, the unity of both body and gaze is splintered and rerouted. His sitters collaborate in the transformation of the studio into a space of queer fantasy. Like Sherman, who shows that reclaiming the apparatus allows one to perform both for and against the camera, Sepuya invites his viewers into a project of imaginative proximity and complicity. They evade the controlling gaze by seducing it, exposing the camera to itself and placing it firmly within a space of shared control and accountability.

TAVIA NYONG'O

THEORIZING PHOTOGRAPHY IN FRONT OF THE CAMERA

James P. Ball / Samuel J. Miller & Others / Frederick Douglass

Man is the only picture-making animal in the world. He alone of all the inhabitants of earth has the capacity and passion for pictures. Reason is exalted and called Godlike, and sometimes accorded the highest place among human faculties; but grand and wonderful as is this attribute of our species, still more grand and wonderful are the resources and achievements of that power out of which come our pictures and other creations of art. Frederick Douglass

Frederick Douglass c. 1841, sixth-plate daguerreotype

Samuel J. Miller, Frederick Douglass, August 1852

Men of all conditions and classes...can now see themselves as others see them—and as they will be seen—by those [who] shall come after them. Frederick Douglass

John Chester Buttre, Frederick Douglass, engraving from a lost daguerreotype, published as the frontispiece to Douglass's My Bondage and My Freedom, c. 1855

Lydia J. Cadwell, Frederick Douglass, 1876, cabinet card

James Presley Ball, Frederick Douglass, January 12, 1867, carte de visite

Frederick Douglass, Library at Cedar Hill, 1411 W Street SE, Washington DC, c. 1893

Poets, prophets, and reformers are all picture makers—and this ability is the secret of their power and of their achievements. They see what ought to be by their reflections of what is, and endeavor to remove the contradiction. Frederick Douglass

Mathew B. Brady, Frederick Douglass, 1877, stereoview

It is evident that the great cheapness and universality of pictures must exert a powerful, though silent, influence upon the ideas and sentiment of present and future generations. Frederick Douglass

Rightly viewed, the whole soul of man is a sort of picture gallery, a grand panorama, in which all the great facts of the universe, in tracing things of time and eternity, are painted. Frederick Douglass

Frederick Douglass, 'Pictures and Progress,' manuscript page of lecture, 1861

FREDERICK DOUGLASS HAS THERE. So often in front of the camera. Allowing himself to be looked at; demanding to be seen; staring down the camera, the photographer, the future. Photographers and technicians impressed his image on surfaces of metal, glass, and paper, drawing it forth with mercury or setting it in silver. They pasted paper prints onto mounts so that others might tuck cabinet cards and cartes de visite into albums and books and frames.

Douglass is still there. And here. The trace of his role in making so many pictures is indelible in this gentleman's dress and deportment, and in his persistent pursuit of the camera. No student of photography's social value as an instrument of American uplift was ever more serious than Douglass. Often described as the 19th century's most photographed American, he undoubtedly approached each sitting with a keen knowing of the visual politics of race, class, and gender. Just as he curated his image in letters across three autobiographies in 1845, 1855, and 1892, he managed his visual image as a race leader and statesman in as many as 160 portraits made from 1841 to 1895, in quiet partnership with scores of photographers, engravers, and lithographers.

Who Frederick Douglass was, then, historians might derive as relying from his photographs as from his autobiographies. For just as these written narratives recall a diverse cast of women and men who abetted Douglass's escape from bondage or supported his rise to national prominence, so do his pictures call up a career of collaboration over his likeness. Douglass understood, like few other sitters, how much the terms of picture-making were a negotiation between the commercial, aesthetic, ideological, and personal interests of photographers, sitters, and viewers alike. In this context, what critics have referred to as Douglass's "self-fashioning" is not an assertion of self-made manhood but an acknowledgment of the important part he played in the production and circulation of his own image as an ex-slave and proud Black American.

Douglass is here, proudly seen. But here he sees, too. The thick event of photography we might see mirrored back at us confirms his witness and authority.

SHAWN MICHELLE SMITH &
MAURICE O. WALLACE

No props, no background, only Douglass's composed presence in front of the photographer who handles the camera that is in between them. 160 images, more and printed in all the available formats of 19th-century daguerreotypes (sixth-plate, quarter-plate, half-plate, ninth-plate, and whole-plate), wet-plate albumen prints, ambrotypes, carte de visites, cabinet cards, gelatin silver prints, charcoal prints, stereoviews, engravings, and lithographs. The first known portrait dates from 1841, the last one, like a testament, shortly after his death, in his home at Cedar Hill, Washington, DC, in 1895. Douglass engaged with approximately a hundred photographers. The names of half of them did not survive, and yet, from the photographs, he seems to have negotiated with them as he did with those whose practice included their signature, about his posture, the format or the decision not to be photographed with ready-made props. These are the people who witnessed Douglass theorizing while sensing the presence of the lens directed at him: C. D. Arnold, J. P. Ball, C. M. Battey, C. M. Bell, D. Bourdon, M. B. Brady, N. Briggs, J. C. Buttre, L. J. Cadwell, R. M. Cargo, T. P. Collins, W. W. Core, A. B. Crosby, C.W. Curtis, L. C. Dillon, J. H. Easton, W. Emory, S. M. Fassett, C. C. Giers, B. E. Hawkins, P. C. Headley Jr., J. H. Hurn, E. B. Ives, J. H. Kent, A. Krecan, J. M. LeClear, S. J. Miller, A. Merand, C. Delevan Mosher, W. Ogilvie, G. Prince, J. Reed, B. F. Reimer, A. H. Ritchie, A. Robin, S. Root, H. P. Rundel, G. F. Schreiber, J. E. Smell, B. F. Smith, J. C. Sundorlini, I. G. Tyson, S. H. Waite, G. K. Warren, W. Watson, E. Webster, E. G. Weld, E. White, C. W. Woodward. Cab.co

---

PLAYING WITH THE CAMERA

Alfred Stieglitz / Irving Penn / Ansel Adams / Todd Webb / Georgia O'Keeffe

I am at last photographing again... It is straight. No tricks of any kind.—No humbug.—No sentimentalism.—Not old nor new.—It is so sharp that you can see the [pores] in a face—& yet it is abstract... It is a series of about 100 pictures of one person—heads & ears—toes—hands—torsos—It is the doing of something I had in mind for very many years. Alfred Stieglitz

When I look over the photographs Stieglitz took of me—some of them more than sixty years ago—I wonder who that person is. It is as if in my one life I have lived many lives. Georgia O'Keeffe

Alfred Stieglitz, Georgia O'Keeffe, 1918

Irving Penn, Georgia O'Keeffe, New York, 1948

Ansel Adams, Georgia O'Keeffe in the Southwest, 1937

Alfred Stieglitz, Georgia O'Keeffe, 1918

Todd Webb, Georgia O'Keeffe, New Mexico, 1945

Alfred Stieglitz, Georgia O'Keeffe—Hands, 1919

Stieglitz photographed me first at his gallery 291 in the Spring of 1917. My hands had always been admired since I was a little girl—but I never thought much about it. He waved head and hands and arms on a pillow—in many different positions. I was asked to move my hands in many different ways—also my head—and I had to turn this way and that...Stieglitz had a very sharp eye for what he wanted to say with the camera. Georgia O'Keeffe

I'm giving her a few lessons with the Leica and she will probably get one. Funny, but she knows nothing of the operation of a camera. She sees well, of course, and seems to have a sense of the photographic eye. Todd Webb

There is the famous wastebasket collection. Stieglitz was making prints and throwing them away, and Georgia [O'Keeffe] rescued them from the wastebasket. So it's called the wastebasket collection. She gave it to us with the stipulation that it would never ever be publicly displayed. Christa Samuels, Beinecke Rare Book and Manuscript Library

TWENTY-FOUR YEARS SEPARATED Alfred Stieglitz and Georgia O'Keeffe when he began photographing her on June 1, 1917. Although to outside observers she appeared to be the celebrated New York photographer and she the rookie art teacher at a Texas Panhandle teachers' college, the power dynamic between them was complex and ever-changing.

She was a feminist absorbed in the writings of Charlotte Perkins Gilman and the suffragist movement—more romantically experienced, with an array of suitors in tow and a career ahead of her. He saw himself as old, impotent, and a failure: "It sickens me to think of myself physically," he had written in February of the year they met. During the subsequent twenty-nine years until his death, she never painted or photographed his face; he had been obsessed with her hands, mouth, and body even before taking a picture or consummating their relationship in 1918. Only slowly did he withdraw his camera, as husband and wife (after 1924) carved out ritualistic rhythms of meeting and separation.

How might we untangle who was the "author" of Stieglitz's groundbreaking portraits of O'Keeffe? He chose her various locations, camera angles, and lighting conditions: in front of her works in the soon-to-be-closed 291 gallery, seated naked but for an opened kimono in the apartment they first shared; grasping the glistening wheel of her Ford or the equine skull that she had brought from New Mexico to Lake George in the 1930s. Stieglitz repeatedly staged her as a fantasy of Eternal Woman and made her the lynchpin of his new concept of the serialized portrait that read character pulsing throughout the body and into the objects that it touched and crafted. She regarded the prints quizzically and, as she somewhat dismissively admitted long after his death, did not recognize herself in the pictures. But when Stieglitz tried these contrived poses with other women, the results were awkward and unconvincing. Successful collaborations, like successful lovemaking, cannot be forced by one person onto another. O'Keeffe's corporeal grace and self-assuredness met a match in Stieglitz's laborious control of every stage of the photographic process.

ANNE MCCAULEY

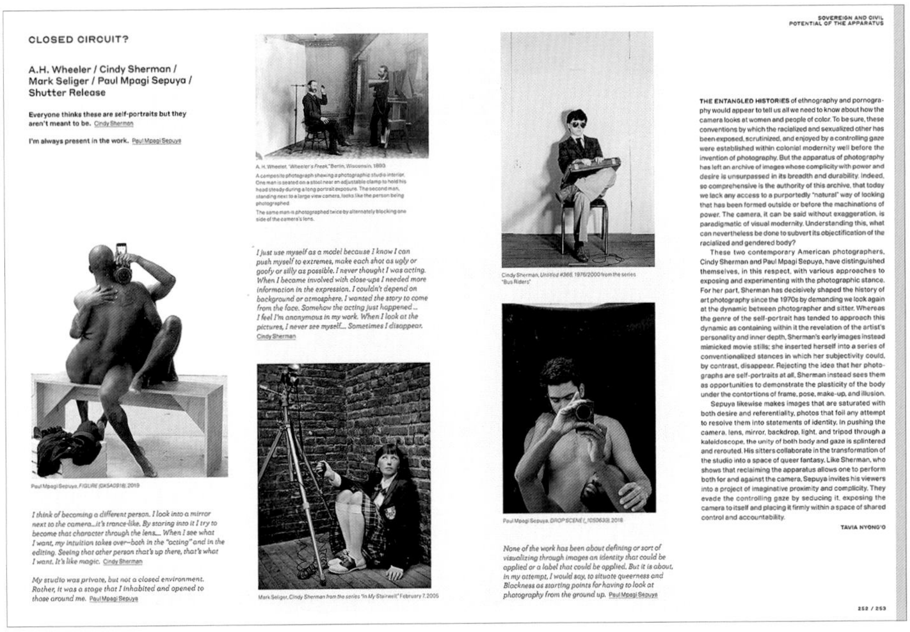

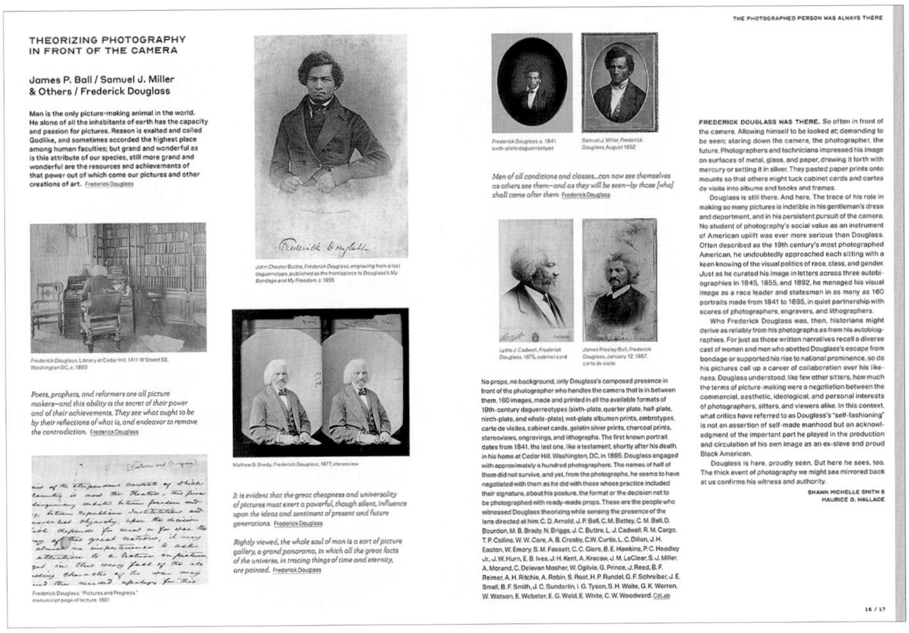

Civil Power of the Apparatus. This de-centring and re-reading of photographers' work was not always easy for the featured image-makers to accept. "When the writing was edited, we always went back to the photographer," says Meiselas. "And there were some who felt that the writers had not understood their work. It was challenging for them to feel not seen in the way that they see themselves, especially if they're more used to being celebrated."

"But that was very deliberate from the beginning, the idea of it being first person from the photographed person, and the photographer, and of having an additional commentary or interpretation or consideration," adds Ewald. "We were trying very hard to keep those balanced, to have the voices come from all sides."

Collaboration picks out some cautionary examples such as surveillance shots by Prague's secret police, as well as more positive approaches, such as LaToya Ruby Frazier's community-based work. But the book is not intended to pass judgement, or even assume an authoritative take. Instead it argues that photographs' meanings are never fixed, and aims to open them up further. It intends to sensitise people to what might be inappropriate, explains Meiselas, but also inspire further questions and a new evolution of work. "It's not a fixed set to be mimicked, it's much more to inspire the next stage of exploration," she says.

Origins of a project

In fact, the project avoided hierarchy more widely, and was put together collaboratively in practice as well as in name. *Collaboration* did not start life as a book, though this form helps spread it; originally it was a collection of interesting photographic projects, which cohered into groups or 'clusters'. These sets were assembled into grids, which the group used with students and workshop participants. Finding that these grids prompted open-ended, thought-provoking discussions, Meiselas, Ewald et al decided to make them more public.

Collaboration popped up as a lab at Aperture Gallery, New York, in 2013, for example, then as a more formal presentation at the Ryerson Image Centre, Toronto. Visitors, students and collaborators were all actively encouraged to contribute, their insights helping build the project and book. One visitor in Canada suggested considering images of nature, and what they say about cameras and their use in surveying and commandeering places, as well as people. *Collaboration* includes a handful of these projects, including Public Studio's *Palestinian Landscapes*.

Meiselas, Ewald, Azoulay, Raiford and Wexler also robustly discussed among themselves, and Meiselas and Ewald point out that they reached a consensus rather than achieving group think; Ewald urges me to watch an online discussion

Left above: *Scherzo di Follia, 1863–66, Oldoini, Countess of Castiglione*. Image by Pierre-Louis Pierson.

Left below: *Sabrina (standing) and Katrina (sitting)*, 2016, from the series *Am I What You're Looking For?* © Endia Beal.

Opposite: *Migrant Agricultural Worker's Family, Nipomo, California, February 1936*. Image by Dorothea Lange.

In print

Collaboration: A Potential History of Photography by Ariella Aïsha Azoulay, Wendy Ewald, Susan Meiselas, Leigh Raiford and Laura Wexler is published by Thames & Hudson, priced £60. thamesandhudson.com

made with Milwaukee Art Museum in 2021, to see that Raiford and Wexler "have their own minds" (Azoulay was unable to attend). It is on YouTube and is fascinating, particularly as it ends and the women swing into a clearly familiar debate. As in my interview with Ewald and Meiselas, they riff off each other and jointly narrate stories, like any group used to speaking together. "I'm laughing because I feel like in our last couple of meetings we just had these ongoing arguments, not arguments but debates, about contact sheets," chuckles Raiford.

"We do have differences of opinion," Meiselas tells me. "That's exactly the challenge. For example, Wendy and I are trying to find ways to wrestle through it [photography and its power dynamics], whereas Arielle is sometimes condemning it fundamentally. We've tussled that together in a number of ways."

Of course, achieving consensus is not easy, and that is one reason *Collaboration* took more than 10 years to complete; in a deeper sense, perhaps, that is why it can never be finished. The introduction to the book ruefully reflects, "we feel we could continue this work for another decade", but the group decided to hand it over so others could continue the discussions "in classrooms, workshops, community centres, in union meetings and at home".

Similarly, the issues and themes are ongoing for the five authors as the introduction also makes clear.

"Our dialogues, practices and conversations with other thinkers and practitioners across geographic locations have generated many meanings of collaboration in all its various iterations – utopic, dystopic, messy, complex," it reads. "We are striving for nuance and inviting questions rather than offering final answers. We continue to learn from the work of others and are engaged in ongoing conversations with those who are included here as photographers, photographed persons, writers and other contributors to the event of photography."

As Ewald and Meiselas tell me, the discussion is also evolving because the media landscape is changing. With digital imaging, the internet and social media, it is no longer only 'hysterics', 'migrant mothers', or young women under forcible arrest who find their images taken and circulated beyond their control. It is all of us – and most of us are also complicit. "It's important, because people with camera phones have absolutely no sense that there is any responsibility," says Meiselas. "There is no social contract at all." **BJP**

susanmeiselas.com
wendyewald.com

QUEER
NEW
WAVE

AS RISING INTOLERANCE INFRINGES THEIR FUNDAMENTAL HUMAN RIGHTS, TRANS AND QUEER ARTISTS ARE USING PHOTOGRAPHY AS A MEANS TO BUILD COMMUNITY, BOTH IN IMAGES AND IN PRACTICE

WORDS BY **GEM FLETCHER**

Opposite: *Ellie, Don't Fear the Queer*, 2022
© Janina Sabaliauskaitė.

"I'M FOND OF THE IDEA THAT QUEERS ANYWHERE ARE RESPONSIBLE FOR QUEERS EVERYWHERE"
BÉRANGÈRE FROMONT

Below: From the series *What's Ours*.

Opposite: From the series *Sexual Fantasies*.

Both images © Myriam Boulos.

On the cover of Myriam Boulos' *What's Ours*, a photobook about power, protest and queerness the artist has been making since the 2019 revolution in Lebanon, a lesbian couple are kissing. Both women have their eyes closed, lips locked, and hold each other tightly as the artist's flash illuminates the landscape of their faces. Boulos spent a lot of time on the streets in Beirut during the revolution – a protest against the government's ongoing corruption and austerity measures, further complicated by the Covid-19 pandemic and the catastrophic port explosion in the city's harbour – and this experience continues to redefine her life and practice.

The image of the couple kissing, the most culturally mobile of the artist's entire portfolio, epitomises how Boulos sees the world: raw, real and up close. She describes the impetus behind the book as "looking for tenderness in a city of destruction", and its central tenet is that intimacy is political. Through her visceral photographs, Boulos reckons with how the body assimilates pain and trauma, and how desire, often our only escape in times of crisis, is entrenched in our political and social realities.

"My friends and I used to take pictures naked in the streets of Beirut," Boulos explains. "It was our way of reclaiming our streets and our bodies. Everything that is supposed to be ours." Portraiture for the artist has always been a way to metabolise the present moment, especially when the issues at hand feel insurmountable. She and her collaborators use the medium to imagine an alternative reality, a space in which they can temporarily feel free. "Photography is about creating a space to exist," says Boulos. "For me, images are a physical space; existing through images is existing physically."

The politics of visibility have long been the purview of portraiture for members of the LGBTQIA+ community, who have used the medium to provide evidence of their love and lives since its inception. As a visual strategy, photography has been a tool for radical coalition and solidarity, building and nurturing self-regard and togetherness. While portraiture as a mechanism may seem deceptively simple to a cis-heteronormative audience, existing through images is not just a survival strategy for Queer people. It is proof of existence in a world in which law and institutions continue to deny our fundamental human rights.

This page: *E11ven in a New York park in summer*, 2023.

Opposite: *Self-portrait*, from the series *Testo Diary*.

Both images © Jesse Glazzard.

"I'M OPTIMISTIC THAT IF THE WORK HAS A WIDER REACH, IT COULD CREATE MORE SAFETY AND UNDERSTANDING ABOUT OUR COMMUNITY, INSTEAD OF DIVISIVENESS"
DEVYN GALINDO

As Boulos' work reminds us, portraiture has been central to the ideology of resistance. Yet, the tension between visibility and safety is increasingly complex, especially in the context of social media, where identities and personal information can be easily accessed. "Since the revolution, I'm very conscious that images can put us in danger," she explains. "It's not the right time to bring the book to Lebanon. In the last month, politically charged, anti-LGBTQIA+ campaigns have drastically reasserted that homosexuality is against the law and the consequence is the death penalty. We've also seen increased attacks by radical groups as intimidation tactics. It's too risky for me and my collaborators to be seen now."

The personal is political

Boulos is not alone in her safety concerns. As I write this piece, the UK prime minister is preaching anti-trans rhetoric at the 2023 Conservative Party Conference, and health bans in the United States are fundamentally altering the material reality of transgender people. This summer, Italy removed the parenting rights of non-biological lesbian mothers, and Hungary instigated a law encouraging citizens to report same-sex families for violating the constitution; meanwhile, parts of Poland still uphold LGBT-free zones.

Despite the many hard-fought freedoms won over the last 100 years, the rise of the far right foreshadows a future in which the LGBTQIA+ community is increasingly marginalised in violent and insidious ways, rendering hyper-vigilance the only way of life. As we approach the end of 2023, where do we stand? How are the politics of representation shifting? How does portraiture function as a care modality? And perhaps most pertinently, what does it mean to make work in an era in which visibility is both liberating and dangerous?

While the representation of the LGBTQIA+ community in culture is evolving, Queer image-makers are rarely recognised for their contribution, and most mainstream storytelling is still told from an outside perspective. "We are fetishised, objectified and routinely targeted by hate speech. How can we possibly build a sense of self in such conditions?" says French artist Bérangère Fromont, who uses her work to reclaim space and fill representational gaps. "I'm fond of the idea that Queers anywhere are responsible for Queers everywhere."

In *L'amour seul brisera nos cœurs*, Fromont's recent book, the artist celebrates dyke identities, creating an "archive of our memories, our imaginations and our dreams for the future". The project, published by À La Maison Printing, presents a monochromatic patchwork of lesbian love through a playful exchange between Fromont's images and poetic texts by Elodie Petit. Focusing on the representation of lesbians at the intersection of several forms of discrimination, the duo use gesture and proximity in their fight against Queer women's erasure in wider culture.

"Not complying with the rules of a heteronormative world is a deeply emotional, sometimes shattering and isolating experience," explains Fromont, who considers photography a space in which marginalised groups can share knowledge and build a survival network. "Staying in the shadows doesn't have to be an obligation. I wanted lesbian love stories to be shown and enacted by people who experience it, for whom it is a physical reality."

For the last four years, Jesse Glazzard has been documenting his transition in *Testo Diary*, a deeply personal exploration of his life after top surgery. Through the images, we witness Glazzard finding himself anew, with the loving support

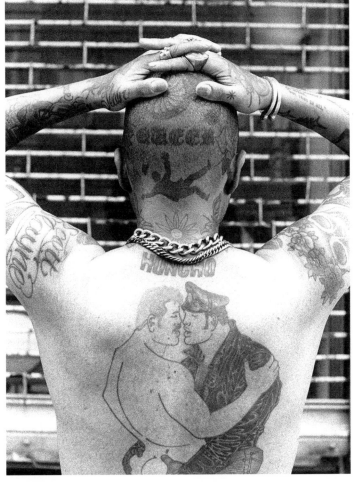

Opposite and above: Images © Devyn Galindo.

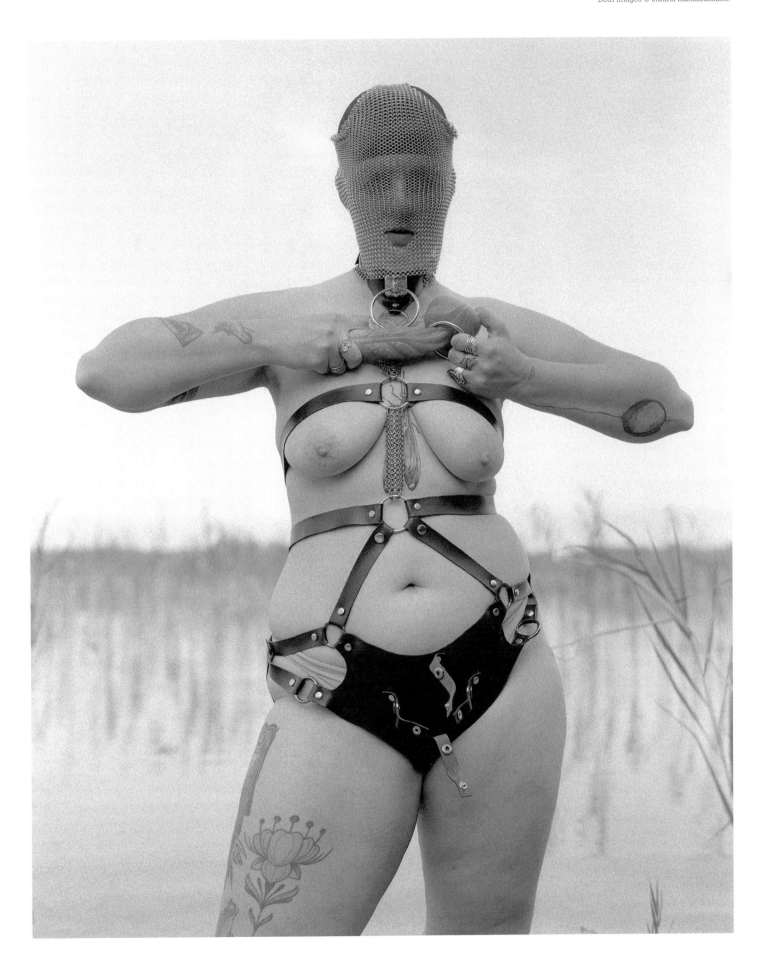

of his then-partner, Nora. The project was initially born out of boredom, during the London-based artist's six-week recovery post-surgery. But over time it became more mission-led, an opportunity to address the lack of trans portraiture in the UK.

"We are living in a weird time," says Glazzard. "We can exist freely but equally face so much backlash. On the one hand, the community is bigger now. It's been powerful to witness the changes in my friends over the years as they are transitioning. But with greater visibility comes risk and hostility." For many individuals, the journey to gender euphoria is not linear, and is deeply affected by sociopolitical contexts. "Some friends take testosterone, then they will go off it briefly. Even for me, sometimes I think I should go back because it's so scary right now. This experience is just one of the reasons why we need to tell our own stories."

Self-portraiture is just one facet of Glazzard's practice. In *Camp Trans*, he collaborates with a community festival that exclusively hosts trans, non-binary and gender non-conforming people in a safe space, encouraging joy and rest from the binary pressures of everyday life. In his latest work, *Soft Lad*, he reclaims the northern slur in a series of luscious portraits of transmasc individuals resting and relaxing at home and in nature.

"I'm only documenting the private spaces of people I'm close with, and most of the time, the work doesn't become public. And if it does, it's consensual," says Glazzard of the delicate ethos of his practice. "I'm not sure I will ever be able to show the *Camp Trans* work, but it felt important to make it." For Glazzard and others, building the archive and centring care in a practice is more important than showcasing the work, though it is work that also explodes our understanding of the linear, contained and sequential conventions of the cultural production of photography.

Create safe spaces

Contemplating modes of display and circulation which best serve the community is also integral to Devyn Galindo's practice. A non-binary Mexihkah transdisciplinary artist based in Los Angeles, they opted to launch their first book in a space in which those who had participated would feel most comfortable. "I feel like I've been very centred on 'by us, for us' from the jump," says Galindo. "I try to keep it more for the community, even to the detriment of my work being seen more broadly."

While these values hold true for the artist, the rising violence across the US is also something they have experienced first-hand, and that has motivated a change in approach. "Right now, the work needs to reach beyond our community because we're living in such an isolated echo chamber; the ramifications of that charted with the rise of hate crimes. I'm optimistic that if the work has a wider reach, it could create more safety and understanding about our community, instead of divisiveness."

In *God in Drag*, a project Galindo has been working on since 2017, they explore their gender journey alongside their transmasc siblings in a multifaceted, intimate series made across the US. Like Glazzard, Galindo's collaborators embody trans joy and speak to a new era of body positivity in which masculine femininity and feminine masculinity are not just seen but celebrated. In particular, *God in Drag* speaks to the sweet and tender friendships accompanying the tougher masculine aspects of taking testosterone, creating a remarkable contemporary portrait.

Galindo sporadically appeared in their previous bodies of work, but in *God in Drag* they centred themself as much as their collaborators, reconfiguring the power dynamics of the work. "I've hidden behind the camera for so long," says Galindo. "The only way to push through this heightened fear is to create work where I can [also] see myself through the lens of my community."

Being vulnerable in front of the camera is just one of the evolving aspects of creative practice for artists such as Galindo. The lateral experience of kin-building is also central, and goes beyond film and photography production to engage with all kinds of community work, from art collaborations to a monthly dance party. "I've been trying to think of all of my life as part of my art practice these days," they explain. "The fear just motivates me to go even harder."

Building community

For Queer artists, manifesting care goes beyond the politics of representation or their photographs alone. It is an intrinsic part of the work. Janina Sabaliauskaitė is an image-maker but also an educator and archivist, who curates festivals and runs a black-and-white darkroom in Newcastle for the Queer community. In her hands, photography is a tool for organising, as well as an act of resistance, reflecting her desire to build safe environments for creativity and play.

"Amazing things can happen when you empower somebody to use a camera or develop film and print pictures," the Lithuanian artist says. "The most important thing is that people have the tools to start archiving their own lives."

In *Sending Love*, an exhibition of Sabaliauskaitė's work at Northern Gallery for Contemporary Art, Sunderland, earlier this year, she presented sensual and erotic collaborative photographs celebrating a sex-positive perspective on masculine femininity – a love letter to her transnational LGBTQIA+ community. The project features Sabaliauskaitė exploring her identity as both an immigrant and gender non-conforming lesbian, and is a provocation to listen to the experiences of Queer folks from a wider geography.

For Sabaliauskaitė, inclusion and collaboration are vital, and she is committed to participating in other photographers' work as much as her own. She hopes this gesture of "building visibility together" will create a chain reaction, helping others feel safe and empowering them to take risks, to push the boundaries of how Queer bodies can be seen and represented. "I always make work with the intention that it will be visible," she says. "First and foremost, because in Lithuania, there isn't much. As Queer people, we can't wait for laws to change; for someone to tell us we can do certain things. We have to take chances, embrace our desires and express ourselves."

If the past is any indicator, the significance of today's visions of Queer life will go unrecognised for years. Yet, these artists instinctively understand how vital it is to create a living archive of, and for, LGBTQIA+ people, and the endless and vital ways in which queerness is experienced and performed. Queer culture, like photography more generally, is entering an era in which the mechanics of cultural production are perhaps more meaningful than the final shot. As we contemplate the role of images in our lives, my focus has shifted from 'Is this good?' to 'What might this do for someone?' **BJP**

@myriamboulos
@berangerefromont
jesseglazzard.com
devyngalindo.com
@janinasabaliauskaite

Got too many books?

DONATE THEM TO SCHOOLS IN THE UK

"Art and Photography GCSE and A-level students are expected to draw ideas and inspiration from a range of contextual sources, in order to develop their own work. Unfortunately, many schools are unable to provide a wealth of resources, such as photobooks, due to shredded budgets and underfunding in state schools."

Rachel Jones, photography teacher in Edmonton, London

Find out more at:
creativecorners.uk

Supported by

British Journal of Photography **BLUE COAT**

EDITORIAL COMMISSIONS MAY HAVE DECREASED FROM THE 1970s HEYDAY, BUT PORTRAITS REMAIN ESSENTIAL FOR CREATIVE DIRECTORS. HERE, **EMMA BOWKETT**, FROM *FT WEEKEND MAGAZINE*; **ANDREAS WELLNITZ**, *ZEITMAGAZIN*; AND **JONNY LU**, *i-D,* DISCUSS THEIR COMMISSIONING PROCESS AND WHAT MAKES A GOOD MAGAZINE IMAGE

INTERVIEWS BY **DIANE SMYTH**

THE COM MSION

MIS-
ERS

EMMA BOWKETT
FT WEEKEND MAGAZINE

FT Weekend Magazine is one of the most respected publications in the UK for commissioned photography, and its director of photography Emma Bowkett has been instrumental in building that reputation. Bowkett is also an associate lecturer at the London College of Communication, a curator, and on the advisory board for the Peckham 24 festival.

I have been commissioning portraiture for the magazine since my arrival in 2010, often to accompany an interview. I tend to keep the brief as loose as possible, so that the commissioned photographer has creative freedom. If the environment is relevant to the story, we will collaborate with an artist who makes work of that nature.

Commissioning is often intuitive. When we published a feature with painter Amy Sherald in conversation with film director Barry Jenkins, I invited fellow American Ming Smith to make the portraits. I have long been an admirer and had been hoping for us to work together, so when this assignment dropped, she was instinctively my first thought – three heavyweight artists in collaboration. The pictures she sent back were fabulous, I think in part because they had a great rapport on set.

Earlier this year, Cindy Sherman had a show in Zürich, and her gallery contacted us with an idea for an interview and exclusive showcase of new work. We are trying out some ways of approaching this format and, because Sherman has been interviewed extensively, we thought it might be interesting to present a feature in her own words. She's an artist who has been addressing the subject of portraiture, self-identity and representation for over 40 years, so we were keen to know what she'd learned and could reflect on in 2023. The resulting narrative was enlightening; Sherman talked candidly about ageing and solitude, AI and kids' self-awareness. It's worth a read for sure. We ran the portraits over 10 pages and a cover.

Recently, I commissioned Jermaine Francis to make pictures for an investigative piece about Sarah de Lagarde, who was injured when she fell onto the Tube tracks in London. Sarah was keen to present as the strong person she is, rather than a victim, and had just gone back to work in the city, so our thought was to make street portraits. Jermaine often works in fashion so we discussed together a visual approach that would reflect this and create something dynamic.

We are a relatively small team on the magazine and an art desk of four, which means we work closely on stories. Editor Matt Vella is integral to this process; he came from *Time* magazine with a passion for visual storytelling. Art director Shannon Gibson will direct the cover shoots, often sending a mood board and discussing masthead positioning and layout specifics with a photographer. We will make a call on studio/location based on the needs of each individual project. I am often working on stories a few months in advance dependent on lead time. That said, we can turn around a story in a matter of hours or days if needed. The magazine goes to press on Wednesday, and we have the hard copy issues back in the office on Thursday morning, which means we can respond to a news story as it breaks.

For me, and for the deputy photo editor Josh Lustig, building up relationships with photographers is essential.

We are keen to work with both early-stage and established practitioners. Photographers will reach out to us directly, or we will make contact. We are both involved in folio reviews and mentorships, and I also teach at universities, so this gives us an insight into new voices emerging onto the scene. We, of course, use Instagram, but word-of-mouth is still an effective way to share ideas. The international photography family is rich and generous in my experience.

We have been fortunate to work with some of the best straight out of college, and watching them evolve is wonderful. Cian Oba-Smith springs to mind here because I began working with Cian after meeting him at his degree show. He has just co-authored *The Portrait Photographer's Manual* with Max Ferguson [page 182]. There's a great passage in the book where he discusses his fascination with the genre. 'I was drawn by making a portrait of someone and was interested in photography as a way of searching for commonalities between people. Most of my personal projects look at communities in some shape or form. I'm particularly interested in the link between the environment and the person, how our environments shape us and our relationships with each other.'

In my opinion, making portraits is one of the hardest things to do photographically. A photo session with a high-profile person can be as short as five minutes so it requires a calm disposition, an organised approach in the pre-production, and most importantly, a creative mind. I have worked with the Dutch photographer Dana Lixenberg several times since I started at the magazine, and consider her to be a brilliant portrait photographer. I have long been curious about her methodology and when we interviewed her in 2022, she generously shared some insight: 'It's not about big gestures or dynamic action. The action lies in small details and the gestures people make without being conscious of them. When you're taking your work – and the person you photograph – seriously and you care, people feel that. It's less about hanging out or being one of the guys. I have to quickly gauge what someone is like or how they are feeling. Sometimes people are a bit defensive at first; maybe they're uncomfortable. It's OK if someone is anxious. It's my job to make the person feel comfortable, not the other way round.'

I remember listening to a talk with British photographer Vanessa Winship in which she discussed her process. She spoke with such gentle humility and grace, it was immediately clear why she's so good at what she does. And I've always been impressed at the research Kalpesh Lathigra will conduct prior to an assignment. He will often draw on his personal experience to find common ground, putting his collaborator at ease. He's another artist with great sensitivity in his work, so perhaps that's at the heart of it." **BJP**

@emma_bowkett

Opposite: Marina Abramovic photographed by Juno Calypso for *FT Weekend Magazine.*

Page 132: Sarah de Lagarde photographed by Jermaine Francis for *FT Weekend Magazine.*

Page 133: Cindy Sherman photographed by Cindy Sherman, in an exclusive showcase for *FT Weekend Magazine.*

"IN MY OPINION, MAKING
PORTRAITS IS ONE
OF THE HARDEST
THINGS TO DO
PHOTOGRAPHICALLY"
EMMA BOWKETT

MAGAZINE OF THE YEAR

FT Weekend Magazine

JUNE 3/4

ANDREAS WELLNITZ
ZEITMAGAZIN

In 2009, Andreas Wellnitz joined *ZEITmagazin*, a weekly publication of *Die Zeit*, Germany's most-read newspaper. The magazine is known for its fresh approach, publishing an issue with 40 different covers to celebrate its 40th anniversary, and commissioning Juergen Teller to contribute a weekly column for a year. Wellnitz also runs his own studio, working with organisations such as LUMA Art Foundation, Ferrari and Nike.

 I'm a magazine guy. I have worked on magazines since 1997, interning and learning everything from scratch. I'm dedicated to editorial, so when I opened my studio in Berlin, I got involved with *ZEITmagazin*. It's been almost 14 years now. The end of the 1990s was a big, big dying-off of magazines – there was the dot.com crisis, there were no advertisements, and *ZEITmagazin* closed after 30 years. Ten years later, when they reopened it, they didn't have an idea how to visualise their content. That was when I got involved, trying to develop how editorial content could be visualised best.

Sending a writer and photojournalist out for a week or two is very rare now. When I started it was like, 'Let's go to Nepal and do something on the Maoist guerillas, shall we send Paolo Pellegrin or Christopher Anderson?' Those days are past. But portraiture is still a huge part of the DNA of *ZEITmagazin*. There is some portraiture on the table every day, we spend hours discussing it.

The portraits we work on vary enormously. A lot depends on whether it's a cover story, because the magazine has a split cover. We can do something over two pages, which means we can play with it. But often it's a bit looser. For instance, recently we had a portrait of the German minister of the interior, Nancy Faeser. I got a call from her department and they were like, 'It's the open day, when the public is invited to visit the ministry, and you can have 20 minutes'. I asked Mustafah Abdulaziz to photograph her, and he did an incredible job. It's all black-and-white, and his authorship made the story.

Portraiture can make the story and the interview feel more true. It's a kind of proof that you spoke to this person, that the text isn't something you made up. If I have someone interesting and I know a certain photographer has a relationship with them, I will try to work with that. I think I have sent Brigitte Lacombe twice to Joan Didion. I don't know how often Juergen Teller has photographed Charlotte Rampling, but there's a magic between them which you can feel. Then I feel like a bystander – I'm just happy these two people are in the same room, and I know everything will be fine. If there's good trust between the person and the photographer, the magic happens by itself.

You can run into situations where you have five minutes in a hotel room, and you will always assign the photographer who is able to bring something home. Or sometimes you will think, 'OK, it's not worth it' – if there's going to be too much discussion beforehand, who is doing makeup, who is doing whatever, or they try to give you PR material. In that case, you look for alternatives. Recently, we had a really long interview with Adele but the photo time was zero, so we did a cover with typography instead.

The worst thing that can happen is that the portrait is boring, but most of the time you're pleasantly surprised.

Sometimes we want to assign someone and nothing works. They're gone, they're on an assignment in Paris and can't be in Berlin on that day. After that you call 10 photographers and they all say, 'I would love to but I can't'. What do you do then? You feel happy if you find someone to do the job!

We also have fashion portraits, which involve huge organisation and a lot of money. We had Usher in the desert once. Then we invest more money, so we try to get these people for a full day. This rarely happens, but we need at least three or four hours. In that case, the budgets are very different.

In the last few years, I have noticed that young people are using an intimate warmth, taking a very personal, deep approach and using it on assignment work. I find it super exciting. I made a book dealing with the sex life of elderly people with Lina Scheynius, and she found a couple who were perfect, very open, and was able to make a bridge from them to her own intimate portrait work, her 'diary work'. Then you have someone like Ren Hang. His work was very staged or opulent, but you could still feel the inner self in it.

We are always looking for new talent, it's exciting to have that mix of established and new photographers. Schools are important – we look at what ECAL is doing, for example, and we have a special relationship with Ostkreuzschule. We worked with Tamara Eckhardt, who graduated from Ostkreuzschule in 2021. But it can also be much looser. Tereza Mundilová was an intern in our Style department – it became clear that she is a fantastic talent and we started working with her. Instagram is another great source.

Often you work with photographers who have assistants, and eventually the assistant asks, 'Can I show you my work?'. Of course, you say yes. Jonas Lindstroem, who is represented by We Folk these days, was a student here and then assisted a lot. We started working with him very early on, and it was always clear that he was a huge talent. We're still working with him when he has time.

You get to know a lot of people. It's a constant exchange of ideas. For me, that's the best way of working together. It's not just being a photo editor, sitting there and looking at a screen the whole day, it's about being in constant dialogue. It's the best part of the job.

In its best moments, working as a photo editor is like being a conductor. You have all these different instruments, all these different volumes and pitches. You have 'he or she will photograph XYZ next week' and you sit at your table and move all these assignments. My work is making the right decision at the right moment for the story, then combining it and planning which portrait comes in which issue. It's all about the mix. It's a lot of fun. I think that's what will keep it alive." **BJP**

andreaswellnitz.com

Opposite: Dance On Ensemble photographed by Jonas Lindstroem for *ZEITmagazin*.

Page 136: Olivia Rodrigo photographed by Tereza Mundilová for *ZEITmagazin*.

Page 137: Jaden photographed by Tamara Eckhardt published in *ZEITmagazin*.

JONNY LU
i-D

Creative director of *i-D*, Jonny Lu looks after the style magazine's cutting-edge fashion, portraiture and documentary photography, including its 'straight-up' head-to-toe portraits. In addition to *i-D*, Lu works on photobooks, record covers, brand identities and advertising campaigns. His most recent project is a series of portraits of young Indian women titled *Narmada*, made with photographer Jamie Hawkesworth in collaboration with British designer Supriya Lele and organisation Girl Rising.

"*i-D* prints quarterly and in each issue we commission up to 10 portraits and 10 fashion stories. Main features are always accompanied by an interview. Occasionally it's just [a portrait on its own] if it's part of a bigger story or around a particular place or subculture. With *i-D* I always wanted the portraits to run quite clean, without too much graphic design or text disrupting them, so often the text runs at the end of a story and we use pull-quotes to tie the images and text together.

The kind of portrait we want, and the number of images, depends on the story. Sometimes less is more and it can be two or three pictures. Usually it's around six to eight. I always brief photographers to shoot some tighter head shots and then some wide 'straight-up' style portraits, which is an easy way to position the subjects into the *i-D* lexicon. Sometimes in the *Eye* section (the magazine's 'eye' on the world), we make a story around a subculture and it's a collage of environmental pictures with portraits, to build a world. I like the idea of a picture of a place also being part of a portrait, to help build the story and give it some kind of visual context.

There are specific parameters the photographer needs to think about when shooting for *i-D*, especially when shooting the cover. I always send page ratio and logo placement for cover shoots, so the photographer is aware of the page proportions and graphic elements. Inside, images are more free, however we sometimes discuss the idea for the layout before the shoot.

i-D has a particular portrait style: the wink. Every cover has a wink. This was a language started early on by Tricia and Terry Jones, the magazine's founders. It stuck because it subverts the idea of a traditional cover portrait and creates a playful intimacy with the subjects. It puts an emphasis on personality, as well as being a binding thread between *i-D* covers over the past four decades. In *i-D*, the 'straight-ups' (or full-length portraits) are the other everlasting portrait style, which is more functional in its purpose of documenting clothing or fashion.

Finding a connection or thread between the subject and photographer is important. Sometimes this is purely aesthetic, and sometimes it's a deeper, more personal connection. With the magazine, it's important to bring the character into the *i-D* world. There's a certain ease and intimacy to a classic *i-D* portrait that we are always hoping to achieve.

I always work with the photographer on the concept to make sure it fits within the context of the issue, and in the broader *i-D* catalogue. We tend to keep things simple and less conceptual. It's more about the character than the set or location. Often there are logistic factors too, especially with the bigger talent. Some artists – and their management – will want to have input. Sometimes the shoot has to be built around an artist's schedule. Sometimes time is short and we just have to find a way to make it work. A photographer can get anywhere from 15 minutes to a full day to shoot the portrait. The bigger the talent, the less time is generally given. But there's poetry in that too. Limited time can lead to great pictures.

There's a certain sense of security working with photographers I have a relationship with. You know what you're going to get to a certain degree and there's safety in that. I also think it's important to nurture new talent and there's an energy in that. Finding a space where both the photographer's vision and the subject's character meet is what makes a good portrait. If it's too one-sided, it misses the mark. A portrait should feel natural and real. I often gravitate towards more 'off' moments than posed set-ups. It has to feel real.

I believe there will always be a need for original portraits in newspapers and magazines. Humans are obsessed with documenting each other and that won't change. But because we are so inundated with images on our phones and social media, an editorial portrait needs to work harder to stand out now. This has led to a lot of hyper-stylised and conceptual portraiture. Ironically, we see fewer classical and simple portraits – which can be much more powerful.

Recently I enjoyed a shoot for *i-D* with the musician Sampha and his daughter, with the photographer Frank Lebon. It was particularly interesting because of a long-standing creative relationship between Frank and Sampha and myself – I designed his album artwork, and Frank photographed Sampha for a magazine called *Beat*, where I was previously creative director. It's nice to grow and develop with other artists and use the magazine as a platform to collaborate." **BJP**

jonny-lu.com

"FINDING A SPACE WHERE BOTH THE PHOTOGRAPHER'S VISION AND THE SUBJECT'S CHARACTER MEET IS WHAT MAKES A GOOD PORTRAIT"
JONNY LU

WE'RE IN NEED OF SOME TENDERNESS LIKE SUNRAYS THROUGH A PASSING CLOUD

New Wave

starring

Sampha

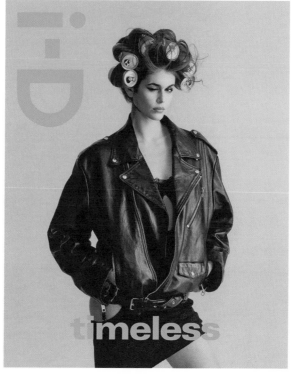

Page 139: Sampha and his daughter photographed by
Frank Lebon for *i-D*.

Top left: HoYeon Jung photographed by Colin Dodgson for *i-D*.

Top right: Kaia Gerber photographed by Tyler Mitchell for *i-D*.

Above left: Bella Hadid photographed by Sam Rock for *i-D*.

Above right: Celina Ralph photographed by Zoë Ghertner for *i-D*.

Opposite: Stormzy photographed by David Sims for *i-D*.

i-D

royalty

Words by **Alex Daniel**

This year's winning bodies of work in *British Journal of Photography's* **Portrait of Humanity include series showing South African men, Berlin women and the Brazilian Tupinambá**

POH
Portrait of Humanity

"Did my mother or my hometown raise me?" asks Lucia Jost. "Maybe you cannot separate these two." Jost's *Capital Daughters* is an intimate portrait of the women of Berlin, a population that includes the photographer. Her work is one of three series winners in *BJP*'s Portrait of Humanity this year, alongside Tatenda Chidora's project on South African men during Covid, and Fernanda Liberti's images of Tupinambá people of east Brazil. Seemingly disparate, these projects all share an interest in community, whether or not each artist belongs to these groups.

Chidora's portraits were made in South Africa and include conversations with his community, tapping into what he sees as a universal experience during the pandemic. Chidora was born in Zimbabwe but now lives in South Africa, and the photographer has been hailed as part of a new generation of artists from across the continent. Fernanda Liberti is a Brazilian image-maker from outside the Tupinambá community, but believes it is important to amplify these people's voices as their way of life comes under threat. She got into photography because of the relationships it can help foster with people outside her immediate circle. "The reason I fell in love with photography was for the connections it brought to my life, and the people from Serra do Padeiro are definitely the most special ones," she explains.

These series have been exhibited at Belfast Exposed and Indian Photo Festival, alongside the 30 single images selected for this year's Portrait of Humanity. All 200 shortlisted single images have also been published in a hardback book by Hoxton Mini Press. Here, *BJP* finds out more about the artists behind the three winning series. POH is an annual survey of the world's faces, in all their variety and common humanity.

Tatenda Chidora
If Covid Was a Colour

Tatenda Chidora's series *If Covid Was a Colour* was made in 2020 during lockdown, inspired by the experiences so many felt during the pandemic – muted angst, frustration and isolation. Visually, however, it could not be more different. The photographer uses vibrant colours and deep contrasts to show models flanked by face masks, or men in hazmat suits against a vivid blue sky. Chidora's output includes fashion photography and he brings a bold commercial sensibility to his portraits.

"The pandemic was a hard and confusing period," he says. "As a visual storyteller, after looking at the imagery that was being published during the pandemic, I was challenged to create a body of work that celebrated mankind's resilience during this time."

Models strike heroic poses, defiant as PPE props surround them; others look timid, pictured in foetal position in one example, but reposed on a deep-blue bed of inflated surgical gloves. Chidora is part of the vanguard of contemporary African artists breathing fresh life into the continent's photographic scene.

"The images represent braveness, resilience, and how patient humans can be in hard times," he says. "Though it seemed like the end at some points, we managed to get through it. The photographs reflect what we experienced, but in a more subtle representation of heroism, and of allowing ourselves to connect with our emotions.

"Besides the pain and loss that came with the pandemic, I feel that the human race needs to be celebrated for adjusting to the hefty shift that came with it," he adds. "This body of work goes on to outline conversations I had with myself and my community, and I hope it serves as a place of remembrance in the future, a celebration of how humans stood the test of time." **BJP**

@tatendachidora

"As a visual storyteller, after looking at the imagery that was being published during the pandemic, I was challenged to create a body of work that celebrated mankind's resilience during this time" Tatenda Chidora

Lucia Jost
Capital Daughters

Berlin-based Lucia Jost turns the lens on the women of her hometown in her series *Capital Daughters*. The work questions the nature of femininity in Germany's capital, and deals with themes such as sexuality, belonging, motherhood and sisterhood. "The myth surrounding the Berlin Woman is complex," she explains. "Who she is, is difficult to grasp. She is considered fearless, sometimes irreverent. She is often called ironic, sometimes sentimental and occasionally grumpy. But then she is also quite different again, and in the end, you never really know. I have often asked myself how I became the woman I am."

Despite being in her mid-twenties, and finishing her photography degree in 2022, Jost is a multi-award winner. She was also a single image winner at this year's OpenWalls Arles Volume 4. "There are so many approaches to speak authentically about femininity," she says. "This one is mine. The project is close to my heart and shows how much the women in my community mean to me. To be able to put them and my work on a big stage through Portrait of Humanity is amazing."

In one image from *Capital Daughters*, a mother holds her baby in the shower, in another two women stand side-by-side in a stairwell wearing matching brown leather jackets. Another woman, heavily pregnant, stares into the camera in what feels like a challenge to the viewer. The project follows on from her previous series *Das Muttertier* (*The Mother Animal*), which explores the mother-daughter relationship while seeking to avoid the stereotypes that often accompany the dynamic.

"The women of my Berlin, especially the mothers of my girlfriends with all their stories, their adventures and influences on the local art scene and subculture, have always fascinated me," she says. "Did my mother or my hometown raise me? Maybe you cannot separate these two. It's not without reason that Berlin is sometimes lovingly called 'the mother city'." **BJP**

luciajost.com

"The myth surrounding the Berlin Woman is complex. Who she is, is difficult to grasp"
Lucia Jost

Dancing with the Tupinambá

Fernanda Liberti's *Dancing with the Tupinambá* focuses on a Brazilian community from Serra do Padeiro, in the eastern state of Bahia, a people who were indigenous to the country before colonial settlers. The portraits feature a Tupinambá woman wearing an elaborate feathered cape, a garment that is sacred to the group.

"In 2020, I started working with Glicéria Tupinambá, artist, political activist and teacher and the first person in centuries to create a Tupinambá mantle – a sacred object that was taken from her people during colonisation," says Liberti. "The portraits were done on the different trips I made to the community as part of our long-standing collaboration and friendship."

Garments such as the cape have existed in Tupinambá culture since at least the 15th century, but were destroyed or stolen by settlers. The cape serves as a microcosm for what happened to the communities during that time, especially as the Tupinambá were once the largest ethnic group in Brazil.

The images now stand as testament to "the sovereignty of [the group's] own narrative," Liberti says. "They possess a strong political and social voice, being an advocate for their rights and land in a country that until recently was at severe war with its indigenous people."

Today, Brazil has its first government department devoted to the issue, the Ministry of Indigenous Peoples, which was established under President Lula. But the country is still recovering from the previous regime of Jair Bolsonaro, who took "a personal stance against demarcation of any indigenous land, like the Tupinambá, where he liaised with local law enforcement and farmers to constantly put their lives in danger," Liberti explains.

"The reason I fell in love with photography was for the connections it brought to my life, and the people from Serra do Padeiro are definitely the most special ones. I was driven to enter Portrait of Humanity to amplify their voices and projects and put the spotlight on them, to help make a more just and equal world." **BJP**

"The reason I fell in love with photography was for the connections it brought to my life, and the people from Serra do Padeiro are definitely the most special ones" Fernanda Liberti

Words and photography by Alice Zoo

Known for his portrait and landscape work, Nadav Kander has a meditative approach in his London studio – and a profoundly subjective take on making images

Nadav Kander

Nadav Kander's Kentish Town studio is bright, with windows on two sides of a large room, its walls made of pale, exposed brick. The feeling is airy and spacious, the surfaces clear. Around the edges, every bit of storage is used to its maximum, the inbuilt shelves dense with boxes of prints, the windowsills adorned with curiosities and ephemera – figurines, souvenirs, a tiny row of books, miniature prints on easels.

A tall, double-sided bookcase is filled with an extensive collection of books, on painting, music and architecture as well as photography. Kander's dog, Juno, lies on a red cushion at his feet, and a taxidermy crow is perched on the desktop monitor. At the crow's feet stands a model Nadav Kander, a homunculus 10 centimetres tall. A quote from Diderot is Blu-Tacked to the computer on Kander's desk, reading "Everything comes to nothing, everything perishes..."

Kander arrived in this studio in 2003, and it was here he developed the work for which he is best known: *Bodies. 6 Women, 1 Man; Dust;* the Prix Pictet-winning *Yangtze – The Long River;* and more recently *Dark Line – The Thames Estuary.* At first his work here was divided between two floors, Kander editing downstairs and photographing upstairs; four years ago, he moved the whole operation upstairs. He speaks of an almost ceremonial connection to the place and his rituals there, especially his work downstairs, "facing south, in a certain part of that studio, with a certain feel of the desk".

The ritualistic process, the creation of the specific, finely calibrated conditions that would provoke the right mindset for the work, was especially defined while he was working on the Thames. "When I made the work on the estuary, I would always arrive in the darkness, onto the river, and I would always leave in darkness," he recalls. "Somehow I never wanted to see real England as I arrived, I wanted it to remain quite mystical.

"And when I did the printing on my computer, and all the relooking at the work, I always came in at three, four, or five in the morning, and would finish by nine. It was always done

"When one is attracted to a great photograph, or great painting, or a great poem, it comes from feeling. When I'm making a portrait, it's the absolute highest percentage of feeling compared to brain. It's almost entirely feel"
Nadav Kander

pre-light, with certain styles of music playing that were quite evocative, and quite dark." (Nivhek's *After its own death*, for example) "I kind of fell in love with that space, and the music, and the early mornings, and very exciting pictures. Because I love the estuary work: I think it's almost the best work I've ever done. It's the most *my* work."

Kander was struck by the bleakness of the estuary when he first went to see it. "I came back a bit dejected, and started making a scrapbook of how other people had seen the estuary, like Whistler, or Constable," he says. Having primed himself with these other interpretations of the river, he was able to see it differently. "It was like I was looking at water that had almost been exhausted," he recalls. "It's slowing down, it's widening, and it's ready to meet its greater whole, the ocean. It's like the end of life, in a way."

For him the river became a moving testament to the "unbelievable human history" it has witnessed on its endless journey through London. "I decided to keep that idea of Constable writing there, unbelievable voyages, people's loves lost, ships never returning, wars fought," Kander says. "And all of this humanness I decided to keep with me in my scrapbook, in my mind, while I photographed."

Working on the images in-studio required another kind of layering, with the river's manifold pasts and histories invoked by involved work on the prints, finessing colour and tone. "The estuary was quite particular in its made-ness," Kander says. "What you're looking at is so bleak, and I wanted them to have a feeling that you're standing in front of a Rothko." To make these very particular prints, reflecting such breadth of feeling and experience, his approach in the studio had to reflect his journeys to the river itself.

"I needed to almost begin again, feeling the same feeling, which is why I would come at night," he says. "I would try to make these works feel like I feel. And that needed layering of colour, or flattening of parts, taking away information where it's not needed, and really getting into printmaking." For Kander, the process was a kind of meditation, "my favourite meditation".

When the work was exhibited at Flowers Gallery in London, Kander included a moving-image work, scored by Max Richter, which showed him sinking and rising beneath and above the diaphanous surface of the Thames, all slowed to half-speed. The film helped guide the viewer's experience of the photographs. "I was talking about the river in old age, softening, darkening, and beginning to die, beginning to be absorbed, and if you would like to think Jung, or Buddhism, you might think evaporate and start again," Kander says. "I wanted the exhibition to become clearer, what it was that I was authoring."

The exhibition asked for more from the viewer than simply contemplating exquisite prints for their aesthetic appeal. "You were here to invite yourself to feel rhythm, to feel tide, to feel this natural phenomenon that is around us, which for me was – is – what this work is about. Being born and dying, another rhythm. And the beauty in that, and the softness of that." In the film, Kander's hands are gently placed above his heart, his eyes closed, face relaxed into a mild and beatific smile. Pulled below the surface, he turns his head, opens his eyes, and looks towards us through the water. Some people left the installation in tears.

This clarity of intent is an absolute priority for Kander. "I'm only really interested in work that shows clear authorship," he says, work that "really shows the person behind the camera". "I remember clocking that when I was a kid, looking at Edward Weston's work," he recalls. "He could show a nude that looked like his portrait, that looked like his shells, that looked like his toilet bowl, his pepper. I remember thinking, 'Five different subject matters, and they all are his'. That was authorship." Kander pauses. "I'm not from the camera club who wants to print exactly what the film has – that's not what it's about for me. I'm much more about how you feel about the shape and colour."

He is frustrated by the narrative around photography, that the medium is truthful, accurate, and somehow objective. "I'm sick of that old school hanging on to reportage, or documentary, and 'storytelling'," he says. Kander believes photographs are as subjective as the paintings and poems he frequently references – in the course of our conversation he mentions Francis Bacon, Marcel Duchamp, Michaël Borremans, Léon Spilliaert, John Constable and Dorothea Tanning.

"I don't photograph to tell stories, I photograph to make stories," he says, quoting from the introduction to his most recent monograph, 2019's *The Meeting*. "Making a story is a bit like Ian McEwan writing a story. He's telling a story but really it's the reader who becomes energised by that, and makes up their own love affair with that book, or how they envisage it. And it's true of poetry too, everybody has a different take on a poem. It's well-known that if you read one, and I read the same one, you might have a very different feeling than me. But photography somehow isn't seen like that, and that frustrates me."

This insistence on clear authorship is intuitive enough for still lifes or landscapes, in Weston's pepper or a river's widening mouth. But Kander applies the same framework when making portraits. Ahead of a portrait session he considers 'How would I show this face if it was a dummy? A Madame Tussauds rendition of the person?'; he also Googles his subject, meticulously plans the lighting, and rehearses so that he and the person can work together to transmit a concentrated, potent and specific feeling. Counter to the way many approach portraiture, for Kander, the subject's own subjectivity is not quite the point. Instead they become an actor, a conduit for something elemental.

The right atmosphere

"I've been jealous of Francis Bacon for a long time, in that he could be in his studio early in the morning, on his own, with his music, cigarette, drugs, whatever, and he would paint from a photograph. He never painted from a person sitting in front of him," says Kander. "It would be so amazing to not have the person there, who has their own agenda. I've got my own baggage, too, I might feel intimidated. I wish I could go and push a mole and they'd just keep quiet for a while!

"People commonly think of a portrait photographer, like myself, making my sitter feel very at ease," he continues. "Talking about how their day has been, so that they become relaxed in what to many people is quite a terrifying experience. A lot of people feel very looked at, very seen – it's a sustained stare. I find that curious. The great portraits that everybody knows and looks at, right back to Rembrandt's self-portraits, where are the great ones where people are super relaxed? Look at Irving Penn's portraits, they have energy and tightness. If you're going to believe in the meeting being truthful, being a true, unmanipulated encounter, then why would I try and interfere with how a person really is?"

It is true that the prevailing narrative around portraiture seems to seek to deny the camera's presence – to coax naturalness, ease and a lack of self-consciousness from a situation that is anything but natural. "Putting people at ease is very overrated," says Kander. His approach is predicated on the artifice of the scenario, the camera, the photographer, the lights. It is akin to the way the artificial setting of a theatre allows actors to present a concentrated version of human stories and emotions and, thus contained, the audience is able to look past the artifice and lose themselves.

Considered response

Kander has a marked determination to hold a space for tension. In conversation he is conscious and exacting, sorting through words until he lands on exactly the right one. At times he stops before a sentence has had a chance to gather pace and pauses to think, completely motionless, as though time is suspended for a moment. His photographs work similarly. They are poised, often melancholic, and profoundly stilled, as though it were life that had stopped the person's motion, not the action of the shutter.

"There's some otherness in me that craves a certain uncomfortable look at things," Kander reflects. "Slightly uncomfortable but beautiful. A bit like putting mustard on chocolate cake." A Jungian might call this otherness the shadow, the yearning towards the unconscious darkness in all of us, the undiscovered, the unresolved. "We all crave it in a way," he continues. "That's why none of us go to movies that show people relaxed, having a nice time, smiling and holding hands."

I ask him about this inclination. Does it arise from the heart, or from the intellect? "When one is attracted to a great photograph, or great painting, or a great poem, it comes from feeling," he says. "When I'm making a portrait, it's the absolute highest percentage of feeling compared to brain. It's almost entirely feel." I begin to wonder about the studio as a kind of therapeutic space, in which feeling is brought up from the depths of the unconscious to be condensed and, ultimately, fixed in a photograph; the lights and gels bringing up the shadow, whether it be Kander's, his subject's, or that of the viewer. "Most of the pictures I've taken," Kander says, "have been without much consciousness of my process at all."

Jung dreamed of consciousness as a house, the conscious mind as the higher floors and the unconscious down lower, on the ground floor, and then deeper still into the basement. Perhaps Kander's studio is like a therapy room, but perhaps too it is like walking into his mind – a first impression of space, the profusion of tiny personal effects like the personality dotted across its edges. The decades-long archive filed into drawers like memories, the heavy machinery hidden behind a curtain, and downstairs newly inaccessible, consigned to the past.

"Probably the main way that [the studio] has informed me is that the mood of how and where I work changed in 2019," Kander says. "When I came upstairs it was just pre-Covid, then right as it all happened, I was moving up. So I hadn't been here that long, and I'm still getting used to the space." His new desk faces the same direction as before, although it is a floor higher – he has ascended, and is newly distant from the depths of his first workspace. "I've never delved as deep as I did when I first did the estuary," he says. "I've still got that goosebumpy time of four in the morning downstairs in my head. I haven't experienced that upstairs yet." **BJP**

nadavkander.com

Who governs what we see in photo museums, foundations and collections? In our Intelligence section, we shine a light on Fotografiska, Nederlands Fotomuseum and a new cultural centre in Lishui. Plus a portrait manual offers practical and ethical tips, a Tish Murtha documentary, photobook highlights and the campaign against online censorship

Intelligence

Body talk

Women's nipples are censored online while men's are not, a state of control that not only reflects society's inequality and discrimination but has worrying repercussions for artists and marginalised groups. Words by Emma Shapiro

Coined in nascent internet days, the phrase 'pics or it didn't happen' has persisted as a prescient motto of the Instagram age. Like its antecedent, 'if a tree falls in a forest...', which predicts obscurity for those not witnessed, this saying equates online activity with actual existence. Since the creation of Instagram in 2010, our lives have become intertwined with social media presence; it has become a tool, a community, and a lifeline for creatives, who have good reason to rely on it.

Natural disasters, financial crises, political turmoil and a pandemic have all contributed to our dependence on a virtual place where we can connect with opportunities and share work. Unfortunately, many artists have found themselves unable to establish that presence, as private companies play the role of arbiter of art and success. For these artists, often photographers, who suffer personal and professional hardship from suppression, erasure and censorship on sites like Instagram, 'pics or it didn't happen' rings ominously true.

Promotional photo from Emma Shapiro artist's book *Cut Out* (2021), removed from Instagram for violating its guidelines.

My first experience with art censorship was not on social media, it was at a Walmart supermarket in rural US. As I waited for a set of self-portraits at the photo desk, the clerk excused himself and a manager replaced him. In a voice loud enough to alert surrounding customers of my indecency, I was told that my prints would be destroyed and that "we usually call the police in this situation". Genuinely surprised and more than a little confused, I pressed the manager who had threatened me, asking why. Eventually, the answer was, "It shows your nipples".

After witnessing my artwork reduced to illicit material for the mere fact that I was a woman and my nipples were showing, I was struck by the sheer inequality of the premise. If a man had taken the same self-portraits he would be walking out with them in his hands, whereas I walked out with only anger and shame. Stalking back to my car, I devised my revenge plot: I would put my nipples everywhere.

One nipple sticker at a time, I would prove that a nipple alone is not just harmless, but genderless. The idea was amusing, serious and popular, and soon it would acquaint me with the boundless joys of art censorship on social media. As post after post was removed for that very same 'it shows your nipples' rationale, I found that my skirmish with content moderation was just one battle in a long war over nudity and women's bodies in art online, a war that has destroyed far more art and artists than any prudish Walmart manager could dream.

Let the fight begin

The first battle began in 2008, when a Facebook group of new mothers grew sick of their photos being removed for 'pornography' and organised a 'Nurse In' at the company's California headquarters. With chants, songs and breastfeeding both in person and online, the 'Lactivists' took a powerful first shot at Facebook's treatment of the female-presenting body.

From the 2008 protest to 2014, Facebook slowly allowed more breastfeeding images, an increase that coincided with rising support for public breastfeeding in the US. Acknowledging visibility to be an influential factor in public acceptance, the US Surgeon General wrote in 2011: "Although focusing on the sexuality of female breasts is common in

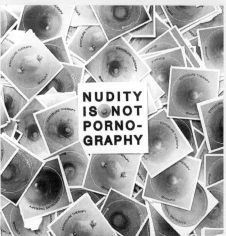

NUDITY IS NOT PORNOGRAPHY

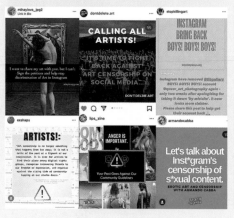

Right from top: Anti-sexist-nipple-censorship protest image from Emma Shapiro's *Exposure Therapy* project @nipeople, 2020; Stickers from *Exposure Therapy*, created by the author; Stickers on display; Instagram posts discussing the issue of art censorship online. All courtesy of Emma Shapiro.

mass media, visual images of breastfeeding are rare, and a mother may never have seen a woman breastfeeding." The coincidence of more visibility on social media and a bump in public acceptance is notable, and suggests that 'real' lives are not just reflected online, but influenced by online interactions.

The correlation between visibility and social acceptance is well-documented, and particularly significant for underrepresented and marginalised groups as it can mitigate stigma and push society forward. In the case of Instagram vs Lactivists, giving visibility was simply a matter of listening to users and adjusting accordingly. This 'win' for breastfeeding sketched out a potentially simple solution for the treatment of marginalised groups on social media – less discriminatory content moderation and an interest in protecting freedom of expression. Despite this, the battle over the female nipple sans baby and the sexualisation of women's bodies has proven not so simple.

In the years following, Facebook (now Meta) cracked down hard on all sorts of female-body related content. The inflexibility of Meta's stance, particularly its anti-female nipple policy, has for years kept artists from changing the narrative around the female body. This has had particularly frustrating outcomes for the photography community, who, despite a heritage of over 200 years, still struggles to be explicitly represented by guidelines that currently state they "allow photographs of paintings, sculptures, and other art that depicts nude figures", without defining what "other art" means.

With Instagram's continual rise as a professional tool, the repeated erasure and censorship of these artists has left them with just a few, unsatisfying options: mar their artwork with self-censorship, keep projects off social media, or change their practice to adapt to restrictive guidelines. The end result is a stagnant representation of the art world, limited opportunities for at-risk artists, and entire bodies of work created specifically with gender-based censorship in mind.

Rise of legal issues

Those who complain about discrimination online are often reminded that private companies make their own rules, and until recently that was pretty much true. Over the last few years, however, a worrisome shift is threatening freedom of expression across the internet, and is particularly concerning for artists who have yet to be welcomed on platforms such as Instagram.

Efforts to regulate the internet and control platforms are being legislated around the world. In most circumstances, particularly in the UK and US, these efforts purport to protect children and vulnerable groups by going after CSAM (Child Sexual Abuse Material) and sex trafficking. Noble concerns, but ones that have fed into surveillance and partisan ideology online. Instagram artists first experienced these effects when, around the start of 2021, they began to receive a violation notification of "sexual solicitation". This new accusation levelled at artwork was more than offensive, it was a signal of something more sinister.

Instagram was responding to pressure from a new US law, SESTA-FOSTA, championed by the powerful conservative organisation NCOSE (previously Morality In Media), which has campaigned against pornography, sex work and same-sex marriage, has supported art censorship and targets women's bodily autonomy. Now Instagram and other platforms became legally liable for anything users posted, spooking them into purging content deemed even potentially illicit, rather than face penalties. This result, when free expression is hindered in an indirect way, is known as the 'chilling effect'. Beyond social media, this chilling effect has also resulted in the termination of artists' websites, online shops, newsletters and payment processors.

> "If a man had taken the same self-portraits he would be walking out with them in his hands, whereas I walked out with only anger and shame. Stalking back to my car, I devised my revenge plot: I would put my nipples everywhere"
> **Emma Shapiro**

Digital-rights groups are sounding the alarm on numerous other impending legal changes, and pointing to the fallout from SESTA-FOSTA as proof of the damage that badly designed and partisan legislation can wreak. Laws that are meant to punish websites for illicit material and surveil users will only push actual bad actors deeper underground and target already marginalised communities, meaning that artists are among the first to be impacted. As digital-rights groups warn of a chilled free expression online, human rights groups are reporting the rapidly increasing rate of art censorship around the world. It is apparent we are seeing a global conservative backlash of anti-sex, anti-LGBTQIA+ and anti-feminist values, and that the online culture we have all grown to depend on is a target.

Many of us fight Instagram because we love Instagram – the connection it provides us to opportunities and each other is unparalleled and we want it equally for all. But Meta has only sat down with artists once and any acknowledgment of its mistreatment of artists has been due to public missteps or embarrassment at the hands of the rich and famous. While Instagram's guidelines correctly note that its policies "have become more nuanced over time", this progress has been too slow.

Real change in the face of rising art censorship will take the combined efforts of a united art world demanding protection for artists and an end to the "needlessly aggressive gatekeeping" online, as described by anti-art-censorship group Don't Delete Art (DDA). The DDA manifesto, which aims to bring these voices together, puts it this way: "As social media companies are held to different and changing regulatory standards in the US, Europe and the UK, it will be critical for at-risk artists to be considered and valued as companies adapt."

With the advent of Instagram and online tools, artists had access to the kind of means and reach they had only dreamed of, an art world finally open to all. In reality though, this access was always obstructed by ingrained sexism and ignorance. Whether torn up in a rural shopping mall or accused of sexual solicitation, art that is restricted by bias will go unseen and artists will suffer obscurity. Through visibility, we can conquer stigma and push our visual narrative beyond the stagnancy we currently risk effecting. Otherwise, if art is not seen, did it ever exist at all? Pics or it didn't happen. **BJP**

Anti-sexist-nipple-censorship protest image, 2022. Courtesy of Emma Shapiro.

Emma Shapiro is editor-at-large at Don't Delete Art, a campaign and resource centre protecting artistic expression across social media platforms.
dontdelete.art
emma-shapiro.com

Dream and do

Nederlands Fotomuseum has a new space opening in Rotterdam in 2025 – thanks to a privately owned foundation, Droom en Daad. Words by Philippa Kelly

From the moment Birgit Donker set foot inside the Santos Warehouse, she fell in love with the space. The eight-storey listed building, located on Rotterdam's Rijnhaven harbour, was everything the Nederlands Fotomuseum director had been looking for in the search for a new home for her institution. The renovated warehouse was so suitable, in fact, that the purchase was finalised six weeks later. Shortly afterwards, the museum announced that it would open there in 2025.

Founded in 2003, following a bequest of 22 million guilders from amateur photographer Hein Wertheimer, the Nederlands Fotomuseum is "dedicated to safeguarding the photographic heritage of the Netherlands". The institution, which receives an annual contribution from the Wertheimer Fund as well as support from institutions such as the Mondriaan Fonds and Dutch Ministry of Education, Culture and Science, holds over six million photographs and light-sensitive photographic objects in its collection. It contains early daguerreotypes and archives of key Dutch image-makers, such as Ed van der Elsken, for example, but also contemporary work by Dana Lixenberg and Erwin Olaf, who died in September 2023.

Since 2007, it has been housed in the Las Palmas business centre, a space which also offers approximately 2,500 square metres for exhibitions, and is rented from a private investor via Rotterdam's local government. But the cost of this space increased by 14.5 per cent over the last year, says Donker, putting heavy financial pressure on the Fotomuseum. The situation was starting to look tricky, until the Droom en Daad philanthropic foundation stepped in, with a €38m proposal to purchase the Santos

Warehouse and give the museum a new home. Set up by a Dutch billionaire family, the Van der Vorms, Droom en Daad currently lists M Van der Vorm as its chair and CO Van der Vorm as its treasurer. "It's an incredible story," Donker says.

Remodelled over more than a decade by German design group Stilwerk, the Nederlands Fotomuseum's new home first opened in 1903; in addition to multiple exhibition spaces, and a large central atrium, it gives the institution permanent facilities to house its collection, a bookshop and library, education rooms, a cafe, and a rooftop restaurant with a panoramic view of Rotterdam. Donker hopes the space will engage local communities in new ways, and elevate the institution to the world photographic stage.

New models

But what excites Donker most is Nederlands Fotomuseum's potential for new forms of display. It will give a prominent place to its current *Gallery of Honour of Dutch Photography*, an exhibition on the story of photography from the Netherlands from 1842 to the present day, and it will continue its existing programme of shows. In addition, it aims to make its collection more accessible. "What we want to do is to make the archive part of the visitor's journey," Donker explains. "It's really strange that in a museum you only see the end product, when it takes so much more to keep our heritage safe for future generations. I think, more and more, museums want to tell the whole story."

She has a point. In 2018, London's Victoria and Albert Museum announced V&A East Storehouse, a 16,000-square metres,

Birgit Donker (right), director of the Nederlands Fotomuseum, and Wim Pijbes, managing director of Droom en Daad, sign the Santos donation agreement © Fred Ernst.

Left: Render of the atrium of the Santos Warehouse, Rotterdam. Courtesy of Renner Hainke Wirth Zirn Architekten & WDJ Architecten.

Below: Exterior of the Santos Warehouse, new home of Nederlands Fotomuseum. Courtesy of Stilwerk.

sector, though that is clearly part of the effort; its stated mission is to "develop initiatives aimed at promoting the arts in and for Rotterdam, to contribute to an even more attractive city for its residents and visitors".

Bloomberg has described the Van der Vorm family as "one of the world's richest and most discreet", but it has long been involved with Rotterdam and with the Holland America Line, founded there in 1873. Bloomberg also reported that the Van der Vorms were linked to a low-tax Dutch Caribbean island in the 2016 Panama Papers leak. But the Van der Vorms are behind the De Verre Bergen Foundation too, a Rotterdam initiative that has put millions of euros into social projects, including food trucks and homes for Syrian refugees.

Degree of autonomy

Droom en Daad's director is Wim Pijbes, an art historian and former director general of the Rijksmuseum, Amsterdam. In a 2018 interview with *de Volkskrant*, Pijbes reported he had had good experiences when working with patrons and philanthropists at the Rijksmuseum, which was one of the reasons he took the Droom en Daad job. He also indicated that he and deputy director Laura Dufour have an enviable amount of autonomy, and Droom en Daad does have a peculiarity – it does not invite applications, instead setting up initiatives or approaching institutions itself.

In this interview, Pijbes also described Droom en Daad as a committed investor, stating that the foundation does not expect financial returns but does want to see social returns, specifically in Rotterdam. In the case of the Nederlands Fotomuseum, the multi-million euro Santos Warehouse came with a stipulation – if the museum wanted to relocate, leaving the people of Rotterdam without access to its images, the building must be returned to its funders. For Donker, this presents little problem.

"Photography deserves a building like this," she says passionately. "It's really an emancipation of photography. Photography was looked down on for a long time, artists discarded it and said, 'It's not art'. This is the crown that photography deserves." **BJP**

nederlandsfotomuseum.nl

purpose-built home for over 250,000 objects, which will offer the public insight into traditionally hidden conservation and restoration practices when it opens in 2025, next door to the new V&A East. In 2021, Depot Boijmans Van Beuningen opened in Rotterdam, meanwhile, billed as "the world's first publicly accessible art storage facility". It is located next to the Museum Boijmans Van Beuningen in the Museumpark, and houses more than 154,000 artworks.

Intriguingly, Depot Boijmans has also received funding from Droom en Daad, and over the last seven years, Stichting Droom en Daad (which translates as the Dream and Do Foundation) has been involved in many other cultural projects in Rotterdam. Set up in 2016, it began supporting the Kunsthal Rotterdam a year later to create an international programme of exhibitions. In 2019, it launched *Over de Kunstbode*, an irregularly published arts and culture supplement, and earlier this year it assisted Art Rotterdam in hosting its first sculpture park, to name just a few of its initiatives.

It is currently working on a project called *Fenix*, in which it will transform a huge warehouse – once the largest in the world – into a story on Rotterdam's history of migration. *Fenix* will include the passenger lists from the Holland America Line from 1900 to 1969, for example, approximately three million records which Droom en Daad has made it possible to digitise, in cooperation with VeleHanden.nl and the Dutch National Archives. Droom en Daad is also working with the City of Rotterdam to improve Het Park, the city park.

Droom en Daad was set up to boost Rotterdam in general, not just its cultural

Collective struggle

How do you make a documentary about a documentarian? Director Paul Sng talks about balancing image, sound and testimony in his film on Tish Murtha. Words by Ravi Ghosh

When deciding whether to take on a project, director Paul Sng asks himself five key questions: What is the story about? Who is the audience? How are we going to tell that story creatively? Why now? What is my right to tell the story? If all have compelling answers, he starts thinking seriously about funding, casting, writing and assembling a team for the film. For *Tish*, Sng's 2023 documentary about the South Shields-born photographer Tish Murtha, the final question was the most important.

Murtha was a working-class photographer with a left-wing sensibility, whose pictures brought a shocking but poetic realism to life in England's deindustrialising north. Her legacy continues through the diligent curation of her daughter Ella, but her work remains less known than that of contemporaries such as Chris Killip and Graham Smith. What would it mean to animate Murtha's life – and pictures – at a time when the cycles of economic inequity and social deprivation are repeating?

Tish intersperses Murtha's photographs with interviews featuring her mentors Dennis Birkwood and David Hurn; friends Ethel Cass and Daisy Hayes; siblings Carl, Glenn, Mark and Eileen; and photographic contemporaries Mik Critchlow and Killip. Many of the conversations are anchored by Ella, who acts as an intermediary between her mother and the contributors, offering personal reflections which steer the narrative. Sng uses Murtha's photographs to illustrate her eviscerating political writings, creating a didactic force while showing the full scope of her practice, from *Juvenile Jazz Bands* to the lesser-known *London By Night*, a depiction of the lives of Soho sex workers.

Some of the most powerful moments in the film occur when Murtha's siblings look back on their own lives in her images.

Glenn describes their father sending the boys out to collect scrap metal, while the camera pans across a picture of a boy standing shrouded in smoke over a molten lead fire. The audience is seemingly caught between eras: the Dickensian poverty shown in the images on one hand and Glenn's memories on the other, balanced by Sng in a single sequence.

Using a documentary format to tell the story of a documentarian presents a paradox. There are several artistic and social perspectives to contend with. "When you're making a documentary, you're beholden to the truth," Sng explains. "Not just your truth – and the integrity of what you're trying to say – but the participants that you're working with." Then there is the truth of the pictures, social conditions frozen in time. The British Chinese film-maker drew inspiration from Murtha herself, he says. She made sure to give a print to all of her subjects, as much an act of courtesy as collaboration. "I try to at least spend a bit of time with someone before turning on the cameras," Sng says. "Knowing that Tish did that informed our process and practice in terms of transparency."

Past lives

Tish is as much a political history as a biography. The film opens with a voiceover in which Murtha surveys her surroundings, her diary entries and writings narrated by the actor Maxine Peake (as in the rest of the film). "High levels of unemployment have always been a hard and constant feature of life in the West End of Newcastle," Peake declares, channelling a conviction as present in Murtha's prose as in her pictures. The young Murtha was a sharp commentator on poverty's ideological underpinnings – the abandonment of a whole generation

captured in *Youth Unemployment* and witnessed first-hand with her own brothers.

"What is becoming clear to the generation now approaching maturity is that our society has no solutions for their problems; can give no direction to their lives," Peake reads. *Tish*'s sound design accentuates these rhetorical moments. A steady drumbeat rises behind Peake's voice as she delivers the lines, turning the observation into a damning judgement. At other points operatic arias soar over the pictures – a nod to the Murtha family's culturally rich upbringing. Carl had ambitions to become an actor; Ella was named after Ella Fitzgerald.

Sng first encountered Murtha's work when editing two photography books: *Invisible Britain: Portraits of Hope and Resilience* (2018) and *This Separated Isle: Invisible Britain* (2021). Ella wrote him a blurb and they began discussing photographers for the second volume. The idea of a documentary about Murtha's life eventually came into focus, with Sng finding an affinity with Murtha's story in his own working-class upbringing. 'It's me and you against the world' was a familiar phrase his mother would use during his

south London childhood, Sng says. He was a young boy when Murtha was documenting the effects of deindustrialisation in the north-east, but his value system closed the distance between them. "I can remember my mum telling me when I was seven years old that Margaret Thatcher was a bad person," he laughs.

Sng's 2021 documentary *Poly Styrene: I Am a Cliché* was made in collaboration with the musician's daughter Celeste Bell-Dos Santos, but his new work was not about searching for another mother-daughter story, Sng says. "It was wanting to make a film about an artist who was an outsider, but was able to challenge the status quo. Somebody who was fierce and didn't compromise, and as a result of that was probably marginalised more than she might have been."

Tish arrives in a films-about-photographers tradition with two distinct formats, while also continuing a lineage of left-wing social documentaries. The elevation of war photographers into hero figures has made them ripe for dramas and biopics, with *Double Exposure: The Story of Margaret Bourke-White* (1989) and *The Killing Fields* (1984) among those centring photographers

Opposite: Stills from Paul Sng's movie *Tish*.

Below: *Glenn on the Wall*, from the series *Elswick Kids*, 1978. Image by Tish Murtha © Ella Murtha.

on screen. A steady stream has continued in the last two decades. *Fur: An Imaginary Portrait of Diane Arbus* (2006) stars Nicole Kidman in a factually imaginative portrayal of Arbus' career, while more recent big-name titles include *Minamata* (2020), with Johnny Depp as W Eugene Smith, and *Life* (2015), in which Robert Pattinson plays Dennis Stock on assignment to shoot James Dean. The fashion-to-war-correspondent narrative also lies behind *Lee* (2023), with Kate Winslet playing Lee Miller.

The documentary format is less glitzy, but allows for a deeper exploration of politically woven stories such as Murtha's (though *Tish* does include a few short, dramatised vignettes, with Murtha played by Shin-Fei Chen.) At several points, Sng creates mixed-media diptychs, showing colour footage of Silver Jubilee street parties and evenings in the pub alongside Murtha's photographs of similar scenes. Recent documentaries have also received critical

acclaim where their Hollywood equivalents
have struggled. David Morris and Jacqui
Morris' *McCullin* was Bafta-nominated in
2012, while the Oscar-nominated *Finding
Vivian Maier* was funded via Kickstarter
shortly after John Maloof began circulating
Maier's pictures, playing a key role in
spreading the word about her work.

In fact, the combination of activism
and artistry makes Laura Poitras' *All the
Beauty and the Bloodshed* (2022) another
antecedent for *Tish*, albeit not an obvious
one. Nan Goldin's activism is inspirational,
as is Murtha's legacy. Exploring Murtha's art
posthumously means that the film becomes
a process of re-activism, the documentary a
microphone for its subject's views. Sng was
drawn to the relevance of Murtha's beliefs
– and anger – today, mentioning UK child
poverty in particular. "What's changed in
that time?" he asks.

Murtha had her own clear ideas about media and motivation. "My use of photography and my approach to it, is based on the conviction that the fundamental value of the medium is its capacity to provide direct, accurate and vital records of the conditions, events and experience that shape our lives," Peake reads from her diaries. This conviction made including Murtha's photographs, and decisions on how to do so, easy, Sng says, adding that Ella had the best eye for placing her mother's pictures.

Murtha was also critical of the photography industry. Killip recalls enjoying support from Northern Arts and Side Gallery, but she received nothing and keenly felt these slights. "This photography world, and those who operate it, really make you sick at times," Murtha wrote after quitting Side. She had felt the gallery was pushing for her work to fit an anaesthetised "philosophy of working-class culture", which she disdained.

Tish is about honouring Murtha's role as part of the community she photographed, Sng says, and she is constituted by others' memories as well as her pictures – deepening the overall portrait and keeping her memory alive. "Presenting Tish as

> **"When you're making a documentary, you're beholden to the truth. Not just your truth – and the integrity of what you're trying to say – but the participants that you're working with"**
> **Paul Sng**

a photographer, an activist and an artist was our mantra," Sng says.

In the latter stages, *Tish* gives way to a moving reflection on Murtha's achievement and death. Ella gently leads the interviewees and the film into more emotional corners, particularly while discussing the impact of her own birth on her mother's career. All agree that Murtha's feistiness dissipated as life took its toll. She was a product of tough times as well as a chronicler of them, and eventually succumbed to the forces her images portray. Ella recounts the anguish of realising that, towards the end of her life, Murtha had not turned the heating on for fear of the cost. And there is pain and anger when Peake reads the job applications Murtha sent to the likes of Sodexo and the local retail centre in her final months. "I like gardening and also grow my own fruit and veg," one reads. "I'm also a keen photographer – and develop my own photos." **BJP**

Further viewing

Tish opened in cinemas in the UK and Ireland on *17 November. Elswick Kids and Youth Unemployment* are available from Bluecoat, priced £22 each.
tishmurtha.co.uk
bluecoatpress.co.uk

Around the world

On 14 September, Fotografiska Berlin opened a six-floor, nearly 5500-square metres space in a historic building in the central Mitte, which includes galleries, cafes, a bar and even a ballroom. Its programming kicked off with three exhibitions devoted to female-identifying artists – Candice Breitz, Juliana Huxtable, and a group show on nudes – and the opening included a performance by musician Peaches. A few weeks later, on 21 October, Fotografiska opened another venue, a four-floor, over 4500-square metres venue in the hip, central Suzhou Creek district of Shanghai. A former warehouse with space for exhibitions, a concept store and a restaurant/bar overlooking the river, it opened with solo shows by Feng Li, Fan Xi, Edward Burtynsky and Samson Young.

Added to Fotografiska's equally impressive outposts in New York, Tallinn and Stockholm, these developments make the organisation one of the largest – if not the largest – private art museum in the world. "I don't know whether we are largest, nor which metrics to measure it by," says

Set up in 2010, Fotografiska is now one of the largest private art museums in the world, with outposts in New York, Shanghai, Berlin, Stockholm and Tallinn. Its executive chair, Yoram Roth, and Marina Paulenka, director of exhibitions, give an insiders' take on the business. Words by Diane Smyth

Marina Paulenka, Fotografiska Berlin's director of exhibitions.

Yoram Roth, executive chair of the board and majority shareholder in Fotografiska Holding. "For what it's worth, we expect to have over 1.1 million guests next year throughout Fotografiska globally."

It is a striking figure, and all the more so because of the speed with which it has happened. Fotografiska's story dates back to March 2010, when brothers Jan and Per Broman opened a venue in the Södermalm district of Stockholm. The Bromans were passionate about photography, having grown up going to their father's darkroom, but nevertheless did things a little differently. The first Fotografiska was housed in an Art Nouveau former customs house and was set up as a destination, not a private gallery, with a bistro, cafe, bar, conference room, shop and event spaces. It did not sell the works on show and it charged for entry and membership. It was also unlike a traditional museum, because it did not hold a collection, and also had no funding, neither from the state nor private donors.

Even so, the brothers made it work and, visiting nearly a decade ago, Roth was impressed. An entrepreneur "with a focus on culture, community and hospitality", he decided to get involved (the Bromans subsequently left). Fotografiska New York opened in 2019, in a landmark, six-storey, 4200-square metres Renaissance Revival building in Gramercy Park; Fotografiska Tallinn opened the same year. The latter is a franchise but, says Roth, is the only Fotografiska run in this way, and it is operated by "friends of the organisation who understand the mission and the brand". As with the other Fotografiska venues, Tallinn's is in a large, interesting building in a cool area, and has a restaurant, bar and events spaces, plus charges for entry. The Fotografiska venues all have an option for membership, a scheme added in earnest with Fotografiska New York in 2019.

In 2021, Fotografiska got together with NeueHouse, a co-working and social membership space with venues in New York and Los Angeles; Fotografiska and NeueHouse were given a parent company called CultureWorks, described as the "pre-eminent global growth platform for culture, experience and hospitality brands". Apparently Roth and then-CEO of NeueHouse Josh Wyatt met at Frieze LA, and recognised they had such similar goals it made sense to join forces. "We realised that we want to be in the same cities, in the same neighbourhoods," Roth told Artnet in 2021. "We realised that the people who are members at work at NeueHouse are the same people who come to Fotografiska after work."

Fotografiska and NeueHouse have since abandoned plans to draw closer – they operate separately, says Roth, and CultureWorks is being wound down. Even so, Fotografiska intends to expand. It describes its Shanghai venue as "its first in Asia", for example, and had plans for a huge Fotografiska London, opposite the Whitechapel Gallery. The latter was shelved in 2020, post-Covid and post-Brexit,

Fotografiska Berlin, at Oranienburger Strasse 54, which opened in September 2023. Image © Bloomimages.

Nudes, one of the opening exhibitions at Fotografiska Berlin, on show until January 2024.

Fotografiska Tallinn, which, like other venues in the group, has places to eat and drink as well as galleries. Image © Fotografiska.

but Roth hopes to circle back to the city, describing London as "the quintessential Fotografiska town".

The organisation also had plans for a Fotografiska Miami, opposite the Rubell Museum, which were much more recently rethought. Roth's take on why is intriguing. "Miami is a great city, but coronavirus led to hundreds of thousands of people relocating to southern Florida," he explains. "It meant that construction costs nearly doubled. The project we had in mind was no longer financially tenable for us. As an independent museum, we receive no state funding, no donations and no grants. We have to be fiscally responsible from day one, so we have to watch every penny we spend."

Global reach

Despite this, Fotografiska is a massive global institution, and its multiple locations give it advantages. Art institutions often hope to tour exhibitions elsewhere; Fotografiska can easily make this happen, its shows able to go to the other side of the world and still remain, in some senses, 'in-house'. It does not happen with all of them though. "Some of the world-famous photographer exhibitions

or conceptual group shows travel to most of our museums," says Roth. "But a lot of the exhibition programming in each house is born from the local community. In New York, Berlin and Shanghai, there are a lot of talented artists and photographers that define our exhibition programme."

Marina Paulenka, director of exhibitions at Fotografiska Berlin, echoes Roth's words. "I'm part of our international exhibitions committee where, with my colleagues from the other venues, we design our rotating shows, our big exhibitions," she says. "But then each of the institutions is curating its own programme... We have a brand that started in Stockholm 13 years ago, so we already had some kind of leadership and direction. But each of our museums has its own local character, and we adjust our programme to our audience's needs."

Paulenka met with locals at least twice a month before Fotografiska Berlin opened, consulting on what the city's cultural scene lacked and what the new venue could add; she says it is an example of "how to build an institution together with your people" and, even programming aside, it has had concrete results. Fotografiska Berlin's exhibition texts

are in English and German, but they are also available in Ukrainian, Turkish and Arabic, because these are spoken by significant minorities in the city. Paulenka would like to add even more languages. Fotografiska also has fast-moving shows, and can therefore respond quickly to social, political and cultural change. "We are not receiving any kind of donations or tax money, and this gives us the freedom to react much faster," says Paulenka.

Paulenka adds that she always makes exhibitions she can stand up in front of, that she believes in and, while Fotografiska does not use the title 'curator', its staff has curatorial expertise. Paulenka is a good example. Originally from Croatia, she founded the Organ Vida festival in Zagreb in 2009, when Balkan institutions attracted little cultural funding, and when she was just 22. In 2018, Paulenka and her colleague Lea Vene won the Lucie Award for the best curator/exhibition of the year, against much older, better-funded nominees. "Our exhibition directors are extremely well educated, but are also deeply embedded in the local scene or tie back into our community," says Roth.

The first Fotografiska, established in Stockholm in 2010. Image © Fotografiska.

Similarly, in preparation for its opening, Fotografiska Shanghai worked with Holly Roussell, an American curator and art historian based for many years between Switzerland and China, who has worked with institutions such as the Musee de l'Elysée, Lausanne; the UCCA Center for Contemporary Art, Beijing; and Museum Folkwang, Essen. Meanwhile, Sophie Wright, executive director of Fotografiska New York since July 2022, was previously global cultural director at Magnum Photos, and worked for Magnum for 17 years. Wright holds an MA from the Courtauld Institute of Art, on which she studied art and patronage and, in a statement released on her appointment, commented that Fotografiska "is thinking about culture and community building in a contemporary way".

Open more hours

Roth for his part talks of "a thirst for a third place, something important between work and home that offers a community", and points to Fotografiska's wider programming by way of an example. These events aim to go beyond "educational moment", he says, so while they might include talks on art collecting, they can also feature yoga classes, sound baths, DJ nights, and stand-up comedy. He also points to a practical difference Fotografiska can make – simply

staying open. "Where we get to make the greatest difference is by being open and accessible at hours when our audience has time," he says. "Traditional museums' opening hours work for school classes, tourists and people who don't have to work. We are able to welcome an audience after work and late into the evening. We are usually open till 11pm at night, and on weekends even longer."

Fotografiska still does not have a permanent collection, and this perhaps pushes the definition of a 'museum' (just as the organisation avoids the job title 'curator' because, as Roth puts it, "the classic 'curation' definition is 'the process of selecting, organising and looking after items in a collection'.") But Roth says building a collection is not the best use of Fotografiska's funds "when trying to fulfil an educational role". "The workshops, talks and classes around our exhibitions are more important," he adds. "I don't see that changing in the future." In fact, it is not so unusual to sidestep collecting. In Europe, a 'kunsthalle' is a temporary exhibition space and a familiar model; in London, The Photographers' Gallery does not have a collection. And while Fotografiska's restaurants, bars and events have raised eyebrows about a trendy 'experience economy', cash-strapped state-funded museums also have them. More traditional institutions also often charge

entry fees, whether to the whole museum or their temporary shows.

It is a moot point because, while this model clearly works for Fotografiska – and is its prerogative as a private organisation – it is also not a reason for all institutions to abandon collecting, which are key archives for future generations. And talk of a 'third space', galleries with a members-only club edge, raises questions about who can access culture (and space) within cities, about ring-fencing and gated communities. Added to this mix is gentrification, a perennial question around cultural institutions, but in this case perhaps extra relevant. Fotografiska can lease fantastic buildings in hip, emerging areas because clued-up property owners like the organisation – and its audience. "Because of the hundreds of thousands of guests that come to our museums every year, we are particularly attractive to property developers who understand what our community contributes to a neighbourhood," says Roth.

This can prove controversial. Fotografiska Berlin has attracted criticism because it is housed in the former Kunsthaus Tacheles, for example, an art squat occupied after the fall of the Berlin Wall. The artists saved the 1908 building from destruction and set up studios and an art centre, but were cleared by the police and bailiffs in 2012. Vestiges of the building's

Opened in 2023, Fotografiska Shanghai is the group's latest addition.

anarchic past remain in its graffiti, carefully preserved by Fotografiska, but the building was bought in 2014 by an investment fund, Perella Weinberg Real Estate. Fotografiska is just one plank of its redevelopment. Residents are currently moving into luxury apartments newly built on the site and, when completed in 2024, the complex will also include a shopping plaza and offices. For some, it is emblematic of a wider malaise in Berlin, and beyond.

Roth has experience with property, and particularly with developing locations through art and culture. Brought up in the UK and US but born in Berlin, he owns and operates the city's Clärchens Ballhaus, one of its last remaining ballrooms. He is also a founding investor in the Genossenschaft für urbane Kreativität, which created Berlin's Holzmarkt entertainment and cultural quarter and the Kater Blau nightclub, and he is CEO of Roth & Sohn, a company set up in Berlin by his father and grandfather, which invested in property such as office buildings, cinemas and bowling alleys. And though he recently left NeueHouse, Josh Wyatt also had connections in property, joining it from Equinox Hotels, where he helped develop what he has described as "a new and innovative hospitality platform in the luxury wellness space".

Fotografiska has in-house business-savvy, which has helped it set up deals such as its recent collaboration with Autograph Collection Hotels, an upscale chain owned by Marriott International. Unveiled in July 2023, the *Impressions* project saw Magnum Photos members Jonas Bendiksen, Cristina de Middel, Gregory Halpern and Alessandra Sanguinetti take up residence in Autograph Collection hotels in Berlin, San Pedro, Oklahoma City and Tokyo respectively, where they shot images (and were themselves filmed for promos). The resulting work was shown at Fotografiska New York, and will head to Fotografiska's venues in Berlin and Shanghai, as well as selected Autograph Collection properties around the world. Fotografiska New York and selected Autograph Collection Hotels properties will also sell prints of the images – the proceeds benefitting the Bronx Documentary Center – and Autograph Collection Hotel guests receive complimentary tickets and discounts to Fotografiska's five global venues. "It has been great to work with organisations that support the arts, and it is important for us to underwrite our various programmes with good partners," Roth says.

Future plans
Bendiksen, de Middel, Halpern and Sanguinetti are all involved with Fellowship.xyz, a platform that sells NFTs, so I ask if Fotografiska is heading in that direction. Roth says he is "an NFT bear",

and that Fotografiska will not be getting involved, but adds that the organisation is very much interested in digital art and the future of images. The word 'fotografiska' means 'in a photographic style', so its remit includes traditional cameras and prints, but also extends far beyond. Samson Young, for example, who had one of Fotografiska Shanghai's opening shows, works with computer programming and video as well as photography and much more besides.

Fotografiska has an eye for the future and that makes it interesting, whether in its approach to photography and programming, or its business model. It is also what draws Roth to China and, he believes, what makes the country a great fit for Fotografiska. "China is a country full of young, culturally curious, open-minded people who welcome a place for contemporary art and culture," he says. "Our global audience is fascinated by what is next and what is new, and a lot of that is coming from the Far East these days. Certainly Korean pop music or movies are having an impact in the west, and we see Chinese photography as a major contributor to the new visual vocabulary. But that process is an exchange and a dialogue, so the chance to show a mix of artists and photographers from around the world in our different museums is our opportunity to inspire new perspectives." **BJP**

fotografiska.com

Fotografiska's American outpost in New York. Image © Rob Tringali.

Visions of China

Investment in a vast new photography centre in Lishui illustrates the scope of the city's cultural ambition, adding to China's stature as a global photographic destination. Words by Diane Smyth

In October 2024, a huge new photography museum is due to open in Lishui, south-east China. The Lishui Photography Culture Center cost 309 million yuan (approximately £34.7million) to build over two years and will have a total construction area of 34,221 square metres, of which 15,150 square metres is devoted to three floors of exhibition space. By way of comparison, the V&A's recently completed Photography Centre in London has 1000 square metres of dedicated space for photography, while New York's Essex Crossing International Centre of Photography, opened in 2020, has just over 3700 square metres of exhibition, education and administration space.

With a population of 2.5 million, Lishui is small by Chinese standards – Beijing has 21.5 million citizens and Shanghai 26.3 million. But it was named the first 'Hometown of Chinese Photography' by the China Photographers Association in 1999 owing to the concentration of nationally renowned photographers in the area, and this inspired the Lishui Municipal People's Government to set up the Lishui International Photography City 10-Year Development Plan. This led to the biennial Lishui Photography Festival, which launched in 2004, and to the more modest Lishui Photography Museum, which opened in 2007 as a place to exhibit, collect and study photography.

"Lishui aims to enhance its cultural landmark and international reputation by promoting the photography cultural brand," says Weixin Fu, director of Lishui Photography Culture Center and the city's Photography Museum, secretary general of the Theoretical Committee of Zhejiang Photographers Association, and a columnist for *China Photography Daily* and *People's Photography Daily*. "Through the medium of photography, Lishui wishes to introduce itself to the world and encourage people to visit and appreciate this city. At the same time, Lishui aims to contribute to social and economic development as well as the growth of the visual industry through the art of photography."

Fu is himself a photographer, specialising in photojournalism. But he has been involved with Lishui's photography institutions since 2013, when he was appointed a key assistant of Wang Peiquan, the director of the China Photographers Association's Curatorial Committee, and a key member of the Lishui Photography Festival Organising Committee. Fu has been actively involved in the planning and organisation of the Lishui Photography Museum and Lishui Photography Festival.

The 2023 festival was held in November. Themed 'Images Gather Possibilities', it included Chinese artists, such as Qingsong Wang, and image-makers from around the world, including big names such as Vivian Maier and Michael Wolf, plus emerging artists. Past festivals have had themes such as 'Images in an Era of Hypermedia', 'Photography as Life', 'Integrate City Life into Nature' and 'New Start from Lishui'.

Since 2019, Lishui Photography Festival has collaborated in depth with the UK's FORMAT Photography Festival, exchanging exhibitions and curatorial programming. In 2021, artist Lingfei Ren was selected to exhibit *From That Day On* at FORMAT in Derby, for example, while the exhibition *un/natural*, put together by the then-

Above: Visualisation of the finished Lishui Photography Culture Center.

Opposite: Image © Zou Jingyao, winner of the Lishui/FORMAT award in 2019.

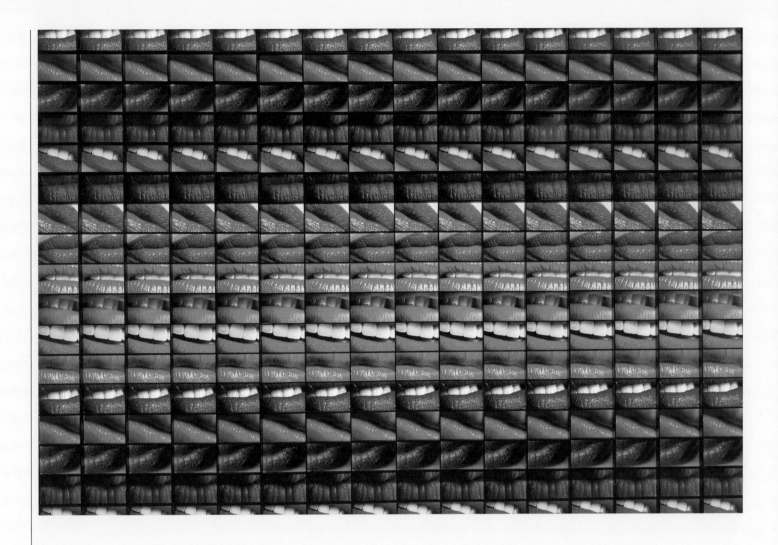

FORMAT curators Louise Fedotov-Clements and Niamh Treacy, introduced to China artists such as Federico Estol (Uruguay), Pietro Lo Casto (Thailand), Jakub Stanek (Poland) and Rosie Barnes (UK). Other external partners who have contributed exhibitions included Yale's MFA Photography graduates and Photolucida's Critical Mass initiative.

"In terms of exhibition planning for the Lishui Photography Festival, we invite professional curators to play a vital role, and we also participate in certain projects," says Fu. "When selecting participating photographers, we consider several factors, such as the exhibition theme, content structure, artistic and topical qualities of the works themselves, as well as the individual identity of the photographers, taking a comprehensive approach."

Deep pockets
Lishui Photography Museum has also established the Lishui International Photography Ranking, a new competition whose inaugural winner will receive an exhibition at the festival and a grant of 1 million yuan as artistic support (just over

£112,000). Again by way of comparison, the award for the Deutsche Börse Photography Foundation Prize – one of the most generous in Europe – is £30,000. As with the Deutsche Börse Photography Foundation, a selection committee nominates photographers to compete for the Lishui award. But in this case, photographers can also apply for nomination themselves.

The judges are experts in various aspects of photography and come from all over the world. The 2023 panel featured Christopher Phillips, independent curator and former curator of New York's International Center of Photography; Gu Zheng, an academic from Fudan University and art director of the Jimei × Arles International Photo Festival 2020–22; Peter Pfrunder, director and curator of Swiss Foundation for Photography; and Sujong Song, senior curator of the National Museum of Modern and Contemporary Art, Korea.

The existing Lishui Photography Museum is an important venue for the festival, and in future the event will move into the huge new centre. The building will obviously be a significant place to showcase photography in Lishui, says Fu, but it will also

allow for more international partnerships. "Its completion is bound to bring more opportunities for cultural exchanges and collaborations in the field of photography," he says. "In addition, we aspire to utilise this platform to introduce Lishui's photography culture and the city to a larger global audience, hoping that it will be well-known and appreciated by people worldwide."

Technological advancements
Fu also organises a photography symposium in Lishui, which runs alongside the festival. Running for the fifth time in 2023, the event focused on the relationship of AI technology and photography, drawing on "the rapid development of AI imaging recently, as well as the continuous redefinition and expansion of people's understanding and perception of art due to advancements in artificial intelligence," he says.

For Fu, engaging with technology is part of the mission, and he says the new centre will provide space to showcase and consider new developments. The 2023 festival, meanwhile, included awards for AI art for the first time. Fu also helped launch the first Photography Art Expo

Top & above: Architectural renders of the centre. Opposite: *No Place to Place*, 2018 @ Wu Guoyong. This work was on show in Lishui in 2018.

(or fair) in Lishui, which in 2022 attracted exhibitors from the imaging industry such as Huawei, Baidu, Philips and Adobe, but also games manufacturers.

"Photography is closely intertwined with the development of technology and the times," Fu says. "Therefore, besides showcasing photographic art, the Photography Center will also focus on the film and imaging industry, as well as technological advancements.

"The centre should have a forward-looking perspective and provide a platform for displaying the film and imaging industry," he continues. "Through the planning and organisation of events such as the World Photography Congress, Lishui Photography Festival, daily exhibitions and professional exchange activities, we hope to offer more opportunities for global exhibitions, collaborations and exchanges within the film and imaging industry. It would be very honourable for Lishui if this platform can contribute to the advancement of new imaging technologies."

As Fu's comments suggest, the photography projects in Lishui also have an eye for business, and another outlet is

> **"Through the medium of photography, Lishui wishes to introduce itself to the world and encourage people to visit and appreciate this city"**
> **Weixin Fu**

the emerging print market in Lishui and, more generally, in China. Fu says he "highly encourages" this market, adding: "Currently, the trading of photographic artworks is well-established internationally, but China started relatively later and primarily focused on first-tier cities. Lishui's involvement in promoting the market for photographic artwork transactions aims to transform art into productivity, enabling more photographic artworks to enter the economic sphere and unleash their full potential value. This endeavour also serves as a positive incentive for artists in their creative pursuits."

Chinese investment

A forward-thinking project with deep pockets, the Lishui Photography Culture Center looks set to firmly position photography in the city, and the city in the photography world. More widely, it helps cement China's position as a hub for the medium. It is part of an ongoing wave of Chinese investment in the infrastructure around photography, which also includes initiatives such as the Lianzhou Museum of Photography. Drawing on the success of the Lianzhou Foto Festival, it opened in 2021.

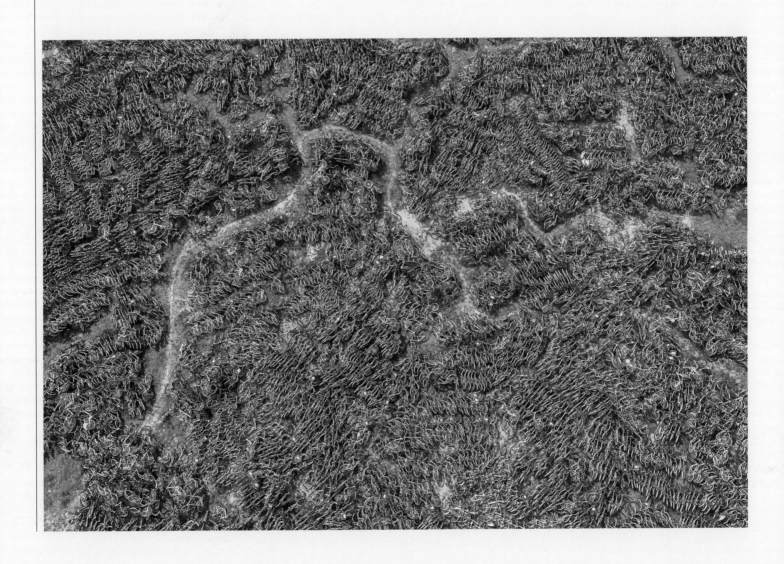

Above: *Self-Portrait*, 1953 © Vivian Maier/Maloof Collection, on show at the 2023 Lishui Photography Festival.

It is fast progress from 2007, when photographers RongRong & inri set up China's first contemporary art space dedicated exclusively to photography and lens-based art: the Three Shadows Photography Art Centre in Beijing. Three Shadows hooked up with Les Rencontres d'Arles, the world's biggest photography festival, to launch Jimei × Arles in 2015, an annual festival held in the port city Xiamen. This year Jimei × Arles is hosting exhibitions by around 90 artists, including by 10 emerging Chinese image-makers selected for the Jimei × Arles Discovery Award. The winner is awarded an exhibition at the following Arles plus 100,000 Chinese yuan (just over £12,000).

Also in 2015, the Shanghai Center of Photography became the city's first museum devoted to lens-based media. Set up by Pulitzer Prize-winning photographer Liu Heung Shing, it is part of an ambitious programme called Shanghai 2035, which aims to transform Shanghai into an international cultural hub through a slew of state funding and initiatives aimed at developing the design, film, performing arts, gaming and publishing industries. It has already helped attract international arts organisations to Shanghai, including the Centre Pompidou, which opened an outpost there in 2020. **BJP**

@lishuiphotographyfestival

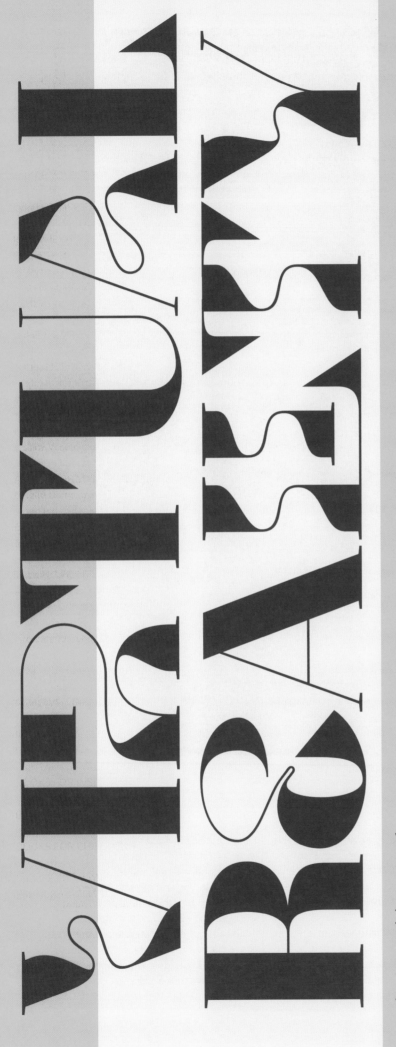

How do we conceive of the world, and how do images shape that conception? The next issue of *BJP* looks at perception, including the impact of pictures in our everyday lives and the ways in which photographers mess with their medium.

We feature **Farah Al Qasimi**, whose work toys with photography's two-dimensionality and the impact of screens and computer games; we also spotlight **Jean-Vincent Simonet**, whose latest series explores the seduction of fishing lures, city lights and advertising assets. And an interview with **Zed Nelson** digs into new work on the Anthropocene, focusing on depictions of the natural world in an era of mass extinctions.

Subscribe via our website
1854.photography/journal
to receive the next issue and future editions

NEXT ISSUE

Guiding lights

Cian Oba-Smith is an Irish-Nigerian photographer brought up in London; born in 1992, he has already carved out an impressive career with his quiet, thoughtful images. His series, on topics such as the legacy of segregation in the US or the notoriety of two housing estates in north London, have been nominated for prizes including the Foam Paul Huf Award and the Ampersand/Photoworks Fellowship, and in 2019 he was the Light Work Artist-in-Residence. His sensitive approach to portraits has also brought him big commissions, from the likes of *FT Weekend Magazine*, *M Le Magazine du Monde* and *The New Yorker*.

Fellow Londoner Max Ferguson has had a similar trajectory. An accomplished photographer in his own right, he lectures at the London College of Communication and is a noted photography director. He is currently photo editor of *Granta* magazine and, prior to that, was photography director of *Port Magazine*, as well as founder of *Splash & Grab*. Oba-Smith and Ferguson's paths have crossed many times, on commissions, joint lectures and workshops, but they have also been friends for a decade. They first met while studying photography at the University of the West of England, and while there realised they had also been to the same sixth form college, a couple of years apart. In fact, they were both inspired by the same photography teacher and in their introduction to their new book, *The Portrait Photographer's Manual*, they give a "Shout out to Miss Miller!".

It is a cute story, but also an interesting insight into their publication. The book has its origins in the many conversations on photography they have had over the last

A new book takes a modest yet radical approach to portrait photography's ethical questions. Its authors, Cian Oba-Smith and Max Ferguson, explain their motivation for making it. Words by Diane Smyth

Kareem, Philadelphia, USA, from the series *Concrete Horsemen*, 2016 © Cian Oba-Smith.

10 years, both as friends and professionals, and it shows. Written in a warm, informal tone, the narrative weaves easily from one to the other, offering different takes informed by a shared perspective on images, image-making and image-sharing.

And the manual is very much a guide, not a coffee-table book, providing approachable but astute insights into ethical problems, working with people, picture editing and even photography kit. "Cheap lights have inconsistent power and colour rendition, which is why we feature examples here that have been lit with natural light, which is free, high quality and almost everywhere," writes Oba-Smith. Miss Miller must be very proud.

Practical tips aside, for Oba-Smith and Ferguson the key motivation was to get readers thinking. *The Portrait Photographer's Manual* was written with emerging professionals, or maybe keen amateurs, in mind but, as they point out, anyone photographing people should be considering ethics, particularly if they are also posting publicly. "With social media, people's awareness of how they're represented has heightened," Oba-Smith tells me. "And with AI and surveillance becoming more

prevalent, it's a dialogue everyone should be having. There's a lot of discussion around protests and the ethics of photographing someone at a protest, for example, if they don't have a mask and law enforcement and the government could use that information. There's a crossover between the artistic world and the public realm, so it's an important conversation to have."

Ferguson agrees, highlighting the significance of ethics in his work at the LCC. Sometimes students feel there are almost no images they should take, he says, but that is not where they should, or ultimately do go with their practice. "In the long-term, thinking about ethics frees people to make work," he says. "That's the point of learning and doing it. It's not to say, 'You can't photograph this person or this community', it's to say, 'I understand the ethical complications and I'm working within them to try and make work that is more collaborative, more inclusive, more representative and, maybe, more willing to slip the power away from me as the photographer and back to the subject and viewer'."

It is a point particularly pertinent to portraiture, they say, because it deals with people, not landscapes or objects,

and therefore involves ethical questions around responsibility and representation. *The Portrait Photographer's Manual* can help put those questions to graduates as they start work, or to self-educated image-makers who perhaps have not heard them raised before. The book includes chapters on photographing family and friends, for example, as well as on setting up portraits in-studio, while chapters on photographing oneself and creating abstract portraits suggest some alternative approaches. There is also a brief history of portrait photography, which picks out some past moral failings. "From mugshots to passport photos, from selfies to surveillance cameras, the relationship between the photographic image and the subject is murky and complex," writes Ferguson.

Ferguson and Oba-Smith offer many insights, but are keen to avoid making hard and fast 'rules'. In fact, photographs can be more interesting when the 'rules' are broken. In a thoughtful analysis of a Gordon Parks shot, Ferguson writes that a foot sneaking out-of-frame is part of its charm, lending the image an air of intimate informality. "So, it is a good portrait, not in spite of the crop but in part because of it," he writes.

Left: *Michelle, London, 2016*, from the series *Woolwich*. Right: From the series *Bikelife*. Both images © Cian Oba-Smith.

Right: Pages from *The Portrait Photographer's Manuel.*

This sense of individuality is inspiring, but it is perhaps where the responsibility also comes in. As Oba-Smith puts it, photography and especially portraiture "is so much about the photographer themselves"; a portrait is a subjective depiction of an individual (or group), so photographers need to think carefully about that subjective reading. "If you have 40 or 50 different photographers photograph the same person, you will have 40 or 50 different versions of who that individual is," Ferguson adds. "And that's just down to the photographer's perspective on that person, it's not necessarily an 'accurate' representation. There is a representation, but you have to consider how a person wants to be represented, and what you're trying to say about them."

The pair raise the question of "intentionality" several times in the manual; the idea that one should make images purposefully, and that such a sense of awareness is what separates portraits from pictures of people. In fact, this understanding underpins the book, with Oba-Smith giving honest insights into his work and how and why he shot it the way he did, as well as his approach to editing and sequencing his images, and how this affects their impact. He talks through a series of portraits of a man called Kareem, which he took for his series *Concrete Horsemen*; he feels the first image was the weakest, he writes, partly because Kareem's facial expression is "too performative". He ended up choosing the third shot because, he adds among other reasons, "his posture exhibits strength, which communicates the feeling I was trying to convey with this series of images".

"It's important to do that [talk about picture editing] because otherwise you look at all the best photographers and you see all these images, one after the other, and every single one's amazing," laughs Oba-Smith. "The reality is that everyone, even your hero photographer, takes shit photos. Everyone does. But it's also important to show that there are the crafted pictures, and how your perspective is put into the image you choose."

The subjectivity of each photographer also comes across in another way: in the selection of image-makers in the book. Rather than simply relying on Oba-Smith's work, *The Portrait Photographer's Manual* includes images by 20 other photographers, including LaToya Ruby Frazier, Zanele Muholi, Jack Davison and Seydou Keïta. These image-makers each have excellent practices but they are also a disparate bunch,

Zanele Muholi
born 1972, Umlazi, South Africa.

Zanele Muholi has described themselves as a visual activist rather than an artist – and when you view their work, it is easy to see why.

Despite the censorship that Zanele Muholi has faced, they have managed to create some incredibly powerful black-and-white portraits that document and generate conversations around the plight of South Africa's Black LGBTQI+ community. Muholi views their work as collaborative, being a member of the LGBTQI+ community themselves and having documented the community since the early 2000s in order to raise awareness of the issues faced by its members.

The self-portrait shown here, titled 'Phila I, Parktown, 2016', draws our attention instantly. Muholi's unwavering gaze locks eyes with us and allows us no respite. It is usual in black-and-white photography to have a broad spectrum of black through to grey and on to white. However, Muholi's decision to use high-contrast black and white makes it seem as if there are hardly any grey areas, an approach that helps highlight the texture of the gloves, with the slightly deflated ones almost looking like human hands. This effect is something of a trademark, consistently appearing throughout their various bodies of work as a stylistic choice.

In this 2017 collection of photographs, 'Somnyama Ngonyama' (Zulu for 'Hail the Dark Lioness'), Muholi created a series of 365 striking self-portraits. The project evolved as a result of a racist incident involving a hotel manager in New York in 2012, which led Muholi to create a self-portrait in their hotel room. This self-portrait then became the catalyst for when they returned to the project in 2014. Muholi made 365 portraits to represent a year of their lived experience. In Zanele's own words, 'You live as a Black person for 365 days. There are a lot of events and experiences that you go through in a year and I wanted to map those important or specific moments.' **COS**

LaToya Ruby Frazier
born 1982, Braddock, Pennsylvania, United States.
latoyarubyfrazier.com

American artist and photographer LaToya Ruby Frazier uses photography, filmmaking, installations and performance as tools for activism. She works on long-term, community-based projects that look at working-class identity in the Rust Belt states of the United States (Indiana, Illinois, Michigan, Missouri, New York, Ohio, Pennsylvania, West Virginia and Wisconsin).

The photograph shown here is from 'Flint is Family,' a 2016 project by Frazier that documents the communities in Flint, Michigan, who were affected by the Flint water crisis. Tens of thousands of people were exposed to dangerous levels of lead in their drinking water when the authorities switched the water supply to the Flint River to cut costs. Thousands of children, who are most at risk of the long-term effects of lead poisoning, including a reduced IQ and increased risks of Alzheimer's disease, were exposed to the contaminated water.

The photographs shown in 'Flint is Family' are split up in the book *Flint is Family in Three Acts* (published by Steidl in 2022) into three 'acts'. Act 1 introduces us to Shea Cobb, a Flint native. She's shown on the left in the image featured here, with one hand resting on her daughter at the front and the other on her mother's shoulder. In Acts 2 and 3 Frazier follows Cobb first to Mississippi to live with her father and then back to Flint to document the installation of an atmospheric water generator.

The question I find so interesting about documentary photography is this: what can photography add to the discourse around real-world issues? For me, Frazier's work is one of the best examples we have of moments when photography actually helps. Through community work, spending time with local people and constant dedication, photographers can make a real difference within communities. By utilizing her position as a renowned photographer, Frazier is able to further conversations around social issues and bring awareness. But I'm not sure that's all her work achieves. The images we see in Act 1 of 'Flint is Family' show protest, community, family, direct action and resilience. They reveal the people fighting for what they should already have. In a more recent body of work, 'The Last Cruze' (2019), Frazier shows us the workers at a General Motors plant in Lordstown, Ohio. It's another place, another state, another community. But the fight and struggles feel remarkably familiar in Frazier's photographs. She is constantly reminding us that the struggles of working-class people against governments that continue to serve the richest in society are sadly continuing **MF**

Jack Davison
born 1990, Essex, UK.
jackdavison.co.uk

Jack is a self-taught photographer who studied English Literature at university, an interest that influences his approach to photography. His photographs are imbued with a kind of magic and have an abstract playfulness that seems to transport you to a parallel universe or a kind of dream state. Jack describes his approach to making pictures in this way: 'You're dealing with things that are in the real world but they're things that maybe only you can focus in on or are excited by. It could be light, it could be a certain person, it could be a certain colour. It's always been about kind of being quite playful with that idea and not getting too absorbed in the theory or the technical side of it, but just the act of making pictures and finding imagery.'

'You can see how Jack's interest in literature has fed into his method for making pictures. Each of his images gives you the abstract ingredients of a story. It's then up to the viewer to navigate the rest of the narrative. As Jack says, 'The most interesting interpretation of the text doesn't necessarily have to be the author's, it can be what the audience or the reader or the viewer brings to it.'

Jack's photographs make you think. Often, you're trying to work out what's going on and how he's created the image you're looking at. The image shown here, for example, is visually a lot more abstract and complex than most portraits. We can tell that the image is a portrait of a person, but we aren't given much more information than that. The purposeful lack of detail in the background leaves the subject's face almost floating in the ether. Jack's techniques with the camera, or otherwise, force us to interpret the image for ourselves. His use of layering and abstraction within the image leaves us with more questions than answers; they leave us questioning who the person is and how this image came to be.

Of his technical process, Jack says: 'Some pictures are made in the moment and it's all done in camera, so shooting through surfaces or catching reflections. Sometimes I like to work [on the images], and I fold those [abstractions] in the post-production, but that's me printing and then rephotographing or shooting screens through a glass. It's a lot to me about adding layers and it's always done physically.'

Think of how you can take inspiration from Jack's approach to making pictures. How can you use layers, perspective, texture and light to create abstract images? Experiment at all points of the photographic process and be critical of your images, but most importantly break the rules and have fun! **COS**

giving a clear demonstration that there are different ways of approaching portraiture. There are Pixy Liao's playful shots of herself and her partner, for example, but then Amak Mahmoodian's thoughtful monochrome images, which function as meditations on the nature of portraiture as much as shots in their own right.

The photographers that Ferguson and Oba-Smith have picked out are also contemporary, reflecting a mix of nationalities, backgrounds and perspectives. That is deliberate, says Ferguson, adding that

> **"In the long-term, thinking about ethics frees people to make work. That's the point of learning and doing it"**
> **Max Ferguson**

they approached image-makers whose work they love, but who also reflected diversity across "all of the metrics we could think of across gender, age, race, class, location, point in your career". "It's people we respect, people who we think deserve it," he says. "But it's also because, when students come to me in their first year, the photographers they name are the same as always – Gregory Crewdson, Martin Parr, and so on. The same names dominate, and are still the only names talked about before you get to university."

Oba-Smith agrees. His education was dominated by those names too, and it took him years to come across others. "Even people like Gordon Parks – when I was learning about photography there was a list of big-name American photographers and he wasn't on it," he says. "It's amazing really. *The Portrait Photographer's Manual* is the kind of book I wish had been around when I was studying photography."

Oba-Smith and Ferguson jointly compiled the list of photographers and say coming up with this dream team was one of the most enjoyable parts of the project. Some, such as LaToya Ruby Frazier, are personal favourites, who they cannot believe they got to work with; others, such as Zanele Muholi, are bone fide contemporary art stars (their work is on show at Tate Modern from June 2024 to January 2025). Some they almost did not approach, assuming they would be turned down or ignored. In the event, nearly everyone readily agreed – testament, perhaps, to the freshness and sincerity of their project.

Oba-Smith and Ferguson worked on *The Portrait Photographer's Manual* for two years, from pitch to publishing. Of that, the writing took about nine months, after many years of discussion. Ferguson says his experience as a picture editor helped them to secure some of the imaging rights, and he is happy they were able to check colour proofs. Originally, though, it was Oba-Smith who was approached for the project. When I ask why he brought Ferguson on board he says simply, "Well, we're friends", then adds he knew the book would be better done together. "Me and Max, we've been having these conversations [on photography] the whole time we've known each other," he says. "This book is really the result of that." **BJP**

max-ferguson.co.uk
cianobasmith.co.uk

From the series *Zanjir*, 2002–2019 © Amak Mahmoodian.

In print

The Portrait Photographer's Manual is published by Thames & Hudson, priced £16.99.
thamesandhudson.com

Reviews by Philippa Kelly, Ravi Ghosh and Diane Smyth

Bookshelf

An ABC of Psychiatry

No Sovereign Author & The Patients of La Fabrique du Pré (Belgium)

The Eyes, €45

According to the *Cambridge English Dictionary*, anxiety is defined as "an uncomfortable feeling of nervousness or worry about something that is happening or might happen in the future", or alternatively as "a medical condition in which you always feel frightened and worried". For anyone who has lived with the sometimes debilitating condition, it is likely that neither interpretation fully captures the breadth of their experiences.

In an attempt to bridge this gap between definition and lived experience, *An ABC of Psychiatry* takes the interpretation of psychiatric terms out of the hands of medical professionals, and places them instead with patients and artists. A collaboration between attendees at Belgium's La Fabrique du Pré day centre and the duo behind No Sovereign Author, Maroussia Prignot and Valerio Alvarez, the book offers a vision of psychiatry rooted in life.

Following the familiar form of a dictionary, *An ABC of Psychiatry* is organised alphabetically, but its pages are not filled with neat lines of uniform text. Instead collages are made up of photographs, paintings and cuttings from medical textbooks, accompanied by scrawled reflections from their creators. Sometimes these artworks speak to a recognisable definition – an image of screaming fans of The Rolling Stones appears as part of the entry for 'hysterical', while 'narcissism' is illustrated, in part, by a woman staring blankly at her own reflection. But elsewhere an image of two firemen battling to extinguish a blaze appears under 'schizophrenia'. It is these less obvious connections that speak most closely to the book's intentions.

Detaching each word from its historical interpretation, *An ABC of Psychiatry* centres the knowledge of the patients involved, and offers a platform for their experiences. Through physically jumbled but emotionally linked images, we are offered invaluable insight into the thoughts of those who experience psychiatric illness – and challenged to reconsider the narrow definitions we ascribe to both people and words. **BJP**

theeyes.eu

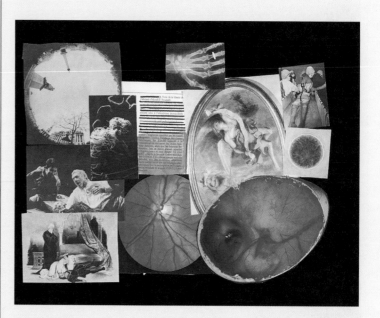

Alcoolisme, from *An ABC of Psychiatry*.

Hunting Heart

Jacob and Sara Aue Sobol

Dewi Lewis Publishing, £45

Jacob Aue Sobol shot to fame when he was in his twenties, after publishing *Sabine* in 2004. Named after his then-girlfriend, who lived in a remote area of Greenland, the book's photographs were made over two years in her village. Gritty and emotive, showing time at home but also the tough realities of fishing in the Arctic Circle, *Sabine* tapped into the Scandinavian idiom of JH Engström or Anders Petersen, but with an intimacy that was Aue Sobol's own. Aue Sobol was accepted into Magnum Photos shortly afterwards, but shied away from publishing such personal work – photographing people in bed, or even making love, but avoiding showing his own life. He also went through periods where he avoided taking pictures altogether, starting to fish again, getting married, and having kids.

Hunting Heart is therefore an interesting proposition, once again finding Aue Sobol photographing those near and dear. It includes Jacob's photographs of his wife, Sara, showing her pregnant or cuddling the kids, as well as the children on their own, and scenes from his everyday life. *Hunting Heart* also includes images by Sara, a talented photographer in her own right, shot on her travels in Russia, US and Mexico. Jacob generally favours inky black-and-white, whereas Sara is given to working in colour. The images are presented as a small box of 24 prints, the couple's photographs displayed in pairs on either side of each card, with an appealing sense of equality; perhaps it might feel intimidating, partnering with a Magnum photographer, but Sara's work stands up alongside his. As for Jacob, it is his work at its best; photographing those close to him with a disarmingly open heart and eye. **BJP**

dewilewis.com

Image from *Hunting in Time*.

Hunting in Time

Ronit Porat

Sternthal Books, $60

Hunting in Time begins with an extended essay by Ines Weizman, founder of the Centre for Documentary Architecture, which sets the scene for Porat's project. Based on her three exhibitions in Israel between 2016 and 2018, it is a "detective yarn evidence board" centred on the murder of a Berlin clockmaker in 1930. Fritz Ulbrich also ran a photography studio at the back of his workshop, making pornographic pictures of young women and girls, and meticulously archiving the results. He was murdered in a robbery gone wrong, by Lieschen Neumann, her boyfriend and a friend. Neumann had been photographed by Ulbrich, adding a layer of scandal to the crime, which helped spread news of it across the continent, and fascinated psychologists, criminologists and sociologists alike. "A murder synchronises multiple narratives and experiences," Weizman writes.

The opening inscription is 'everybody knew' accompanied by one of Ulbrich's portraits, a woman clasping her hand across her chest in a striped dress. What follows is a compilation of archive photographs, first in assemblages which Porat calls 'index sheets', and then in sparser, more associative arrangements. Pictures of women blur and fold into image ephemera drawn from contemporary psychiatric, jewellery and surgical instrument catalogues, as well as early designs of corsets and chastity belts. Also interspersed are photographs by Martin Munkácsi, August Sander, Clare Strand, Batia Suter and Francesca Woodman; all bearing the shadowy, ashen palette which gives the book its visual continuity.

The scope of Porat and Weizman's research is where the book's achievement lies, though the essay's length and historical details – though absorbing – at times unbalance the volume, adding a thick layer of prescription which draws attention from the archives. There is no resolution or "solving of the puzzle" here, Weizman reminds us. Instead, *Hunting in Time* lies somewhere between a sociocultural study of the ominous late-Weimar period and a captivating archive presentation, which reflects this time of intrigue, suspicion, visual innovation and shifting morals. **BJP**

sternthalbooks.com

Image from *EV3RY(TH1NG'5)_MOV1NG: BUT_IM (STILL) H3RE.*

EV3RY(TH1NG'5)_ MOV1NG: BUT_IM (STILL) H3RE

Ibrahim Azab

Folium, £20

EV3RY(TH1NG'5)_MOV1NG: BUT_IM (STILL) H3RE is a reinterpretation of Azab's 2019 magazine-based collage work *FOPDTMM,* but a slower, more deliberative intervention. The book features photographs of paper offcuts and trimmings, often arranged in sculptural forms in which rips, tears and gaps become deliberate invitations to speculate on boundaries and utility. The images are laid out in a traditional photobook format, including double-page spreads, offset crops and plenty of blank space. This design encourages us to understand paper not just as a compositional material, but as a photographic subject in itself. "It's about seeing without being seen," Azab says cryptically, in curator Rodrigo Orrantia's short accompanying text.

Several images in *EV3RY(TH1NG'5)_ MOV1NG: BUT_IM (STILL) H3RE* nod to Azab's position as an artist of assembly, best demonstrated by his ongoing *Hyperdeath-Drive (HDD)* series. But those digital collages rely on a digital recontextualisation and recoding of familiar objects: AirPods, a bike tyre or disposable coffee cup estranged by their inclusion in his synthetic prints. This book, on the other hand, creates a contrived alienation between page and viewer by keeping a strict focus on paper itself. What are we looking at? And will turning the page offer us more information – the typical model of accumulative, left-to-right reading – or will we instead be confronted by a new mode of thinking about materiality?

The puzzle-style envelope which encases the A5 volume is the first clue that the book will continue the self-referential method that defines Azab's practice. Images of cutting boards feature throughout, a nod to the book-making process at a time when artists' studios – albeit typically painters' – are being romanticised and seen as sites of art historical significance. The importance of tactility and, crucially, trial-and-error to book and printmaking is referenced throughout, processes in which remnants, scraps and dummies are as important as the final artefact. "Is that the paper, or the image?" is Azab's opening query. This book does not offer an answer, but instead multiplies the question. **BJP**

folium.site

The Rice is on the Hob

Tony and Tami Aftab
WePresent, £38

Tami Aftab and her father grew up in vastly different parts of the world. While Tony Aftab spent his formative years in bustling, inner-city Lahore, Tami spent hers in west London – one of the city's more genteel areas. Throughout the pages of the pair's co-authored photo-slash-cookbook, these varied connections to their cultural heritage take centre stage, as does their shared passion for food, and their love for each other.

The Rice is on the Hob is a book that father and daughter dreamed of for many years. Throughout her childhood, Tami found that food offered the strongest connection to her Pakistani heritage; as author Jyoti Patel writes in the book's poetic introduction: "One mouthful takes you back to a thousand moments already lived. Your body stays here, in London, but your mind is in Lahore." For Tony, who has experienced short-term memory loss for more than a decade, it is the recollections – and recipes – of dishes from his youth that have endured.

In February 2023, the pair finally returned together to Lahore, and began creating images for The Rice is on the Hob. Brightly coloured, sometimes overwhelming cityscapes speak to the disorientation that Tami felt in the unknown and yet somehow familiar city. Tender, intimate portraits of the photographer's father illustrate the strength of her connection to her family, and her ancestral homeland.

Woven between these images are the recipes of Tony's childhood. Printed on paper more reminiscent of a notebook than a photobook, and accompanied by handwritten notes, a family history can be sensed between the measurements, timings and instructions. These recipes are designed to be torn from the book, to be passed on and used to forge new connections. Despite this, the volume is not truly a cookbook but rather a love letter to food – the memories it can hold, and the important role it can play in lives lived across two cultures. **BJP**

tamiaftab.com

Image from *The Rice is on the Hob*.

Plastic Flowers

George Maund
Self-published, £35

Every now and then, a new image-maker appears and their name immediately gains traction. George Maund, a recent University of the West of England graduate, is a good example. Having previously shown in a graduate exhibition at the Arnolfini and in group shows at Serchia Gallery and the Royal Photographic Society (all in Bristol), his series was one of the standouts at Fold, a 2023 summer graduate event organised by the UWE tutors at Copeland Gallery, London. His images also featured in *Common Ground*, a book published by Vessel Editions in August, and at London's Photobook Cafe in November, in an exhibition of work of the South West Graduate Photography Prize shortlist. In addition, Maund has published a very limited-edition book of his UWE final project, *Plastic Flowers*.

Maund has an aesthetic that is popular at the moment, as *Common Ground* shows. It is a collection of delicate black-and-white shots by emerging photographers, all focused on the natural world (the tagline is 'An Ode to the Forest'). There are some particularly striking images by Iollann Ó Murchú, Luke Spencer and Jodie Wilkins (one of the book's publishers, along with Sam P Cashmore

and Lyle Ingram, also talented artists). But Maund is one of the most striking, with two images taken from *Plastic Flowers*.

His series has a strong conceptual base, exploring his "relationship to the construction and performance of forms of masculinity" through staged imagery with close friends and family, and depictions of scenes and spaces in which ideas of masculinity are questioned and reimagined. It is an interesting topic handled in interesting ways. Maund's photographs of plants and landscapes do not seem immediately on-topic, but then consider the Barbican's 2023 show *Re/Sisters* and its links between ecology and gender, which draw on theories of ecofeminism – the idea that women and the natural world have both been exploited by a capitalism yoked with patriarchy. The argument is valid, but, as *Re/Sisters* also shows, men too have been exploited and stereotyped. To move forward to a more balanced future, with each other and the planet, men and the masculinity expected of them also need a fundamental rethink.

Maund's images suggest a different way of looking at men, a more sensitive regard for something softer – moving and familiar, yet seldom displayed. It is perhaps surprising that this work is by a man in his early-twenties. What is less surprising is that Maund's name is recurring. It will doubtless pop up again in the future, and where his work goes is something to watch. **BJP**

george-maund.com

Image from *Plastic Flowers*.

Engage and Destroy

Jason Koxvold

Gnomic Book, $42

A British photographer based in Portland, Oregon, and upstate New York, Koxvold takes a cool look at his adopted country. His work circles around the US military and prison systems, considering the culture which produces and underpins these institutions and the effect they have on society. His 2017 book *Knives*, which features an essay by Stanley Wolukau-Wanambwa, is a deep dive into New York State's Hudson Valley, an area dominated by the Schrade knife factory until 2004, when it closed suddenly, putting 700 people out of work. A maximum-security prison became the town's biggest employer, but it continued to decline, with drug abuse, mental health crises, and white nationalism all rising.

A sister publication, *YWRAA (You Were Right All Along)*, collated monologues from some of the characters in *Knives*, featuring business letters and online comments. The images in it were located using military grid references to Bagram, Afghanistan; sniper training camps in Utah; the site of a mass killing in Las Vegas, and more. These books suggested something about violence and competition, about a dream of opportunity that has turned red in tooth and claw.

Engage and Destroy picks up on the theme. Made at Fort Moore, Georgia, between May 2021 and 2023, it depicts male US Army recruits at the beginning and end of their basic training cycle. The results of this training are not easy to detect, though a few of the men do look thinner. Perhaps the point is that the training is not visible, because in the centre of the book is a more shocking section. The carefully posed portraits break down into stark monochrome in documentary shots of hand-to-hand combat in which the men are sweaty and injured, grappling and choking. Here is competition at its most raw, yet the men still appear put-together in the colour portraits. In the US, the military is still celebrated, its soldiers heroes.

A text taken from the *Soldier's Creed* runs underneath the black-and-white reportage with lines such as "I will never accept defeat" and "I am an expert and I am a professional" sounding alarmingly similar to both war cries and motivational mantras. As elsewhere in Koxvold's work, what is suggested is a common mindset which underpins both combat and capitalism. **BJP**

gnomicbook.com

Lick of tongue, rub of finger, on soft wound

Keisha Scarville

Mack Books, £45

Lick of tongue, rub of finger, on soft wound is a great title for a photobook – intriguing, impressionistic, and near-collage in effect, much like Scarville's images. The cover is literally a collage and there are similar works and layouts inside; the image sequence also combines Scarville's striking monochrome shots with archival images, family photos, and even an X-ray of a jaw. Within her photographs are multiple layers too, heavily patterned fabrics piling on top of each other, the black-and-white film and the 2D effects of photography combining to dizzying effect, or showing the ravaged surfaces of rocks.

Scarville's work is conceptually layered and polyphonic, combining popular culture with references to her Guyanese heritage in the fabrics and her sparse texts. "To jump the fire three times/To bend towards the sun/To clap roti/For the couch to absorb your scent," reads one, a prose poem that stretches across a spread.

Born in 1975 in Kings, New York, Scarville has studied at Rochester Institute of Technology, and taught at Bard College, New York University and Parsons School of Design. In *Lick of tongue, rub of finger, on soft wound*, her sophistication and technical skill are clearly on show. The monograph strikes an intimate, emotional chord, the images of fabrics recalling an earlier series, *Mama's Clothes*, in which she photographed herself wearing her deceased mother's dresses. Scarville covered her face in those images, as if in mourning too deep to show, and there is a similar sense of melancholy here, plus the same decision not to show faces in her own work.

Lick of tongue, rub of finger, on soft wound also features aspects of *Black Backstage*, an essay by poet Harmony Holiday which picks up the anonymous theme to consider the right not to be seen. "We understand departure not as some maudlin tragedy that threatens to undermine a governing codependency, but as our resistance to overexertion, and refusal to waste energy on static or leak life force into a vat of chaos and trend," Holiday writes. "The Black backstage is where we go when we disappear." **BJP**

mackbooks.co.uk

Children by Markéta Luskačová

Interview by Diane Smyth

Playground, Pointers School, London, 1988
© Markéta Luskačová.

Born in 1944 in Czechoslovakia, Markéta Luskačová graduated with an MA in sociology then went on to study at Prague's FAMU (Film and TV School of the Academy of Performing Arts). From 1970 to 1972 she photographed theatre performances at the Divadlo za branou, then in 1975 left Prague for England. Luskačová shot street markets in London, beaches in Tyneside, everyday life in Ireland, and children – a constant theme in her work. In 1977, she had a son, Matthew Killip. Luskačová has exhibited at institutions such as Side Gallery, V&A, Whitechapel Gallery, Tate Britain, MoMA and the Martin Parr Foundation. More recently, her work was on show at Stills in Edinburgh, where it was accompanied by a catalogue, titled *Children*, produced by Bluecoat Press.

How did you get into photography?

It was while I was studying sociology at Charles University, Prague. My first photographs were of pilgrims in Slovakia, and my professor thought I could combine photography with sociology, suggesting my images could be part of my thesis on traditional Slovakian religious festivals. It was during the Prague Spring, a good period in my country's history – I couldn't have graduated with this theme a year earlier or later. My finished thesis consisted of the photographs and a sociological text. I realised that, for me, photography opened a profound way of understanding people and life.

You started making images around the time of the Soviet invasion of Prague, 1968. What impact did this event have?

Rather than photographing the tanks in the streets, I photographed people's reactions to the invasion – the sad and bewildered faces of the citizens, women crying and hugging, people praying, the vigils and funeral processions for youngsters killed by Soviet soldiers. The invasion affected everybody. People who protested against it lost their jobs; many left the country, including Josef Koudelka and my sociology professor.

Prague's theatres were centres of dissidence, particularly Divadlo za branou. How did you work there?

When Koudelka left, I succeeded him as Za branou's photographer. Otomar Krejča [the founder and director] staged Sophocles' *Oedipus-Antigone*, expecting it to be their final production before the communist authorities closed them, in the aftermath of the invasion. He invited me to exhibit *Pilgrims* in the theatre foyer, explaining he was trying to convey a similar message with the play as I was with my photographs – people acting on their beliefs, regardless of the consequences. It was my first exhibition. Krejča taught me about the responsibility of the photographer, constantly reminding me that, when their performance ended, my photographs would be the only things left.

Why did you photograph street markets and street musicians in the UK?

I was an immigrant, without any of the social connections that are so important in Britain. Outdoor events were more accessible. But I started going to the markets simply because I needed to buy things as cheaply as possible to survive. I took photographs while shopping. I wanted to remember the faces of the traders and their customers, their vivacity and their fortitude. By photographing them, I was also speaking about myself.

You have photographed many children, why is that?

Photographs of children permeate my work.

At home I have pinned up a quote from *Limping Pilgrim*, by Czech writer and painter Josef Čapek, who is more eloquent than I could be: "I love children very much and I respect them greatly. I am overwhelmed by their divine urge to scoop up life and to be loved... [their] joyfully wild need to be alive, the power of growth acquiring and conquering life endowed with astoundingly optimistic energy, enabling them to stand to the absolute supremacy of destruction that rules over all things."

Have you ever felt pigeonholed as a woman photographing children?

No, it was always known I photographed other subjects. But it helped me make a living. Men, I was told, did not like photographing children, and good picture editors know there is a better chance of good work if photographers like what they photograph. But a few curators were always too busy to come if I invited them to see my photographs of children. I feel lucky that Ben Harman, director of Stills, did not consider the subject unimportant, and I could exhibit my photographs there.

Was it difficult to keep photographing after becoming a mother?

Yes. Being a single mother, a freelance woman photographer and an immigrant was not easy. [But] I didn't give up. I kept taking my own pictures, that nobody commissioned or paid for, despite life's difficulties. **BJP**

bluecoatpress.co.uk